Perfect Strangers

Perfect Strangers

*True Stories and Secrets for
Finding Your
Soul Mate on the Internet*

Susan L. Buckley

Writers Club Press
New York Lincoln Shanghai

Perfect Strangers
True Stories and Secrets for Finding Your Soul Mate on the Internet

Writers Club Press
an imprint of iUniverse, Inc.

For information address:
iUniverse
2021 Pine Lake Road, Suite 100
Lincoln, NE 68512
www.iuniverse.com

ISBN: 0-595-24942-6

Printed in the United States of America

To Larry
Once a perfect stranger;
now my perfect soul mate and life companion.
You mean everything to me.

Contents

Acknowledgments

My first words of thanks and gratitude belong to God. I believe that all of the good in me, and in each of us, and all of our actions that produce good, come from God who is the Divine within us. I have no doubt that it was God who put the idea for this book in my mind and delivered the means to write it, just as He brought my husband Larry into my life. It's my sincere hope that God's love and desire to provide each of us with earthly love in the form of a mate, reach all who read *Perfect Strangers*.

I am amazed and touched by the couples who were willing to share their personal stories. Without them, there would be no book. Their courage and generosity of spirit is unbelievable. "Thank you" doesn't adequately express my gratitude for their contributions. Hopefully this preservation of their love stories will be enough.

I'd like to thank my parents, Harold and Kathryn Larson, for modeling and instilling in me a love of reading—a necessary seed to plant for the growth of a writer—and for being an inspirational and concrete example of a life-long love relationship. Thank you, too, to my daughter Kate for sharing her knowledge of the Internet with me, and to my youngest daughter Sarah for not complaining when I fed her cold cereal for breakfast and quickie dinners when I was busy working on the book.

My friends Melanie Crawford, Marcy Mackey and Maureen Fischer, and my other mother, Sarah Buckley, were instrumental through their constant encouragement and belief in me, as was my long ago therapist Anne McGlaughlin, who pressed me continually to do what would make me whole and what I was meant to do: write.

Without my nail technician Raiden Berglund, this book would never have been written. It was she who urged me to move outside my comfort zone and try a new way to meet men—on the Internet. She taught me the ins and outs of Internet dating including steering me to the personals site where I met Larry. Thank-you Raiden.

Additional thanks to the women in my writers' groups for their invaluable suggestions about the book and writing critiques: Susan Armstrong, Maureen Fischer, Bonnie Graves, Jan Hoffman, Janet Johnson, Fran Klete, Deb Sweeney and Alice Vollmar.

And finally, this list would not be complete without recognizing Robert Lawrence Buckley. Larry, you and our relationship have been the inspiration of *Perfect Strangers*. You are my partner in all possible ways. Your copyediting of this manuscript is evidence of this and another example of how well we work together as a team. The countless hours you put into making *Perfect Strangers* what it is today, and your endless love, support and encouragement fill me with gratitude and wonder at how I could be so blessed to have found such love with you.

Preface

The conception of *Perfect Strangers* occurred as serendipitously as the path that led me to my true love. It was nearly Valentine's Day 2001. My boyfriend Larry Buckley and I had been exclusive for nearly a year. America Online (AOL), my Internet provider, was promoting the movie *Sweet November* with a Valentine's Day contest. The rules were simple: in 25 words or less, tell how you met the love of your life. The prize was a romantic trip for two to New York, where the movie was filmed.

I titled my entry *Internet Love*. After submitting it, I wondered if it really went through so I typed in "Internet Love" and hit "Search." Up popped a hundred or so entries from people all over the country who had met the love of their lives on the Internet. They were all AOL members so their screen names and e-mail addresses were listed with their stories. I started reading. Almost no one paid attention to the 25 word limit. Some of the stories were a page or longer. They were interesting, but more than that, heartwarming and some of them, amazing. After I read a dozen or so, I realized what I needed to do. A voice inside my head was insistent. "Publish a book about couples who met on the Internet like you did and share their stories to inspire others and give them hope in their search to find love."

I hit "Print" and instantly had a hundred contacts. I sent them all an e-mail with the subject line "Sweet November Contest." My text read: "Hi. Your love story for the Valentine's Day contest caught my eye. Like you, I met the love of my life on the Internet. I'm writing a book about couples who met on the Internet and might want to include your story. If you're interested, please contact me before February 20."

Almost everyone replied and most in the affirmative. Many of the couples said they felt it was important to let others know that there is hope and love out there. Others wanted to dispel negative notions that some people have about the safety of the Internet or the kinds of people who choose to meet others there. Most of the couples in the book have elected to share their real names, hometowns and photographs. A few have asked that only their first names be included, and I have honored those requests. Only a few of the couples I contacted refused to share their story. No matter. There were many others who were willing to trust a stranger and to share their personal stories in great detail. Perhaps it is that trust and faith in the good of mankind that attracted the soul mates they had been searching for all their lives.

Perfect Strangers has some "secrets"—a few basic how-tos—about Internet romance. Its primary purpose, though, is to instill hope in its readers by sharing the inspiring stories of real couples who found love on the Internet, sometimes under the most surprising circumstances.

Susan Buckley

Chapter One

Basics of Online Romance

Why Online Meeting and Romance

Ask almost anyone what one thing they wish they had more of and their answer will probably be either money or time. We are all busy, too busy; it's a phenomenon of the 21st century. Online meeting and courtship address that concern.

The Internet allows communication with an infinite number of people without leaving home. Instead of spending an hour getting ready and then several hours at an event where you may or may not meet anyone who interests you, you can sit at your computer in pajamas, with dirty hair, munch on tortilla chips, and meet your soul mate.

Many say that meeting the right person is just a numbers game; kiss enough frogs and you'll eventually find your prince (or princess). Some say meeting your soul mate is fate. As the couples' stories in *Perfect Strangers* reveal, the Internet satisfies both the realist's and the romantic's desires. It provides access to thousands of eligible singles along with a healthy dose of fate. Match.com, one of the leading matchmaking online sites, reports approximately 500,000 members with more than 1,300 confirmed marriages and hundreds of thousands of relationships.

The Internet offers an element of control over whom you meet, and at the same time provides a bit of mystery, a necessary element for a romantic spark. Increased personal control coupled with an infinite number of possible love connections and a dose of serendipity make this setting more exciting and successful than meeting in traditional ways.

Some feel that an additional advantage of meeting online is that the important first impression is usually based on personality or compatible interests rather than physical attractiveness. E-mailing or instant messaging, is similar to the nostalgic tradition of letter writing, when people got acquainted with the spirit before the physical.

And finally, you will meet people online whom you would have never met otherwise. One of them could be your soul mate.

Proven Ways to Make the Connection

Placing a personals ad, chatting in special interest rooms, meeting on game sites or special interest boards are the primary ways to meet others online.

Placing a personals ad allows you to be specific about who you want to meet. Those who answer your ad will probably fit most of your criteria (although women have been known to subtract a few pounds and years, and men to add to their height and income). Chapter two explains in minute detail the nuances of writing an ad. I have been more detailed in this area of meeting online, as this is where my personal experience and knowledge lie.

Meeting in a special interest area (chat room, game site, message board) leaves more to chance, fate, and serendipity although you share at least one interest with the others you meet. However, chatting online requires you to be more computer savvy and possess a quicker wit and speedier typing skills than meeting through an ad where you have the luxury of time to compose your response.

The Author's Internet Love Story: *Perfect Strangers*

"Still, in spite of ourselves, our relationship had its own agenda and dying wasn't part of that."
Susan Buckley

The last place I ever expected to meet the love of my life was on the Internet. Although a writer by profession, I hated computers. I also resisted change, especially when I thought it might disturb my creative flow.

It had taken me years to switch from scribbling my first drafts in longhand to using a typewriter, and more years before I reluctantly replaced my typewriter first with a word processor and finally a computer. Although I used a computer on a daily basis, I was and still am, to put it kindly, technophobic.

In the fall of 2000, my computer use was limited to my computer's word processor and an occasional search on the Internet. This abruptly changed when a French manicure appointment challenged my attitude about computers and ultimately altered my life.

It had been a year since my divorce and I confided to my nail technician Raiden that I was having a hard time meeting suitable men. "I've attended a divorce support group and gone to at least half a dozen church socials and singles dances and I haven't met a man I've wanted to talk to for more than 10 minutes, much less date," I complained. I added that I was thinking of signing up with an expensive dating service even though they didn't guarantee a certain number of introductions or satisfaction.

In her early 20s, Raiden, both single and dating savvy, loves to give her clients advice. "Try the Internet; that's where I meet all the men I date," she suggested. "It doesn't cost anything and I've met a lot of great guys." She went on to explain that there were many sites on the Internet where I could place a free ad and she gave me the names of two: OneandOnly.com and Digitalcitypersonals.com.

Free sounded a lot better than spending a couple of grand so I spent an hour writing my ad and placed it on the two sites. "Salubrious, Sparkle, Substance" read my headline, one which I hoped was enticing enough to encourage contenders to click on it and read my ad:

Adventurous Scandinavian writer with child-like passion for life seeks male companion to share the journey. I am 48 but am told I look 10 years younger. My interests include reading; hiking; ice skating; theatre; quiet evenings at home cooking, playing Scrabble or listening to favorite CDs in front of the fireplace; weekend explorations; early morning hours. I love snowstorms, windstorms, thunderstorms, the constellations, random acts of kindness to strangers, birch trees, the North Shore, teaching, learning, giving, receiving, playing, laughing, crying and sharing. I dislike smoking, arrogance and passivity. You are a health-minded individual; a person of integrity, honesty, passion, kindness; a life-long learner who knows himself, his priorities, is living an authentic, abundant life and loves the journey.

It's common knowledge in the online personals world that women over 40 receive significantly fewer responses than younger women. In addition, personals sites claim as much as an 80 percent increase in responses for those posting a photograph with their ad.

Although I wanted as many responses as possible, I couldn't change my age and I chose not to include a photo. Although I'm considered attractive by most people, I wasn't interested in men who would decide whether or not to meet me based on my looks, and I liked the element of mystery that meeting without a photo provided. I was prepared for a meager response, perhaps one or two dribbling in every few weeks or so. Two days later I was stunned after receiving more than 60 responses to my ad.

Sixty men is a lot of men to meet. I tried the conventional ways of meeting men for months and hadn't met one man I was interested in. Two days on the Internet and at least 50 of the 60 men who answered my ad sounded great—at least on paper. They were well-educated, normal-sounding nice men who thought they fit my criteria and were looking for the same things I was. They didn't appear to be wacko, psycho or desperate. They included engineers, lawyers, business owners, a doctor, architect, banker, pilot and high school basketball coach. Good news, right? Sure, until I realized that even if I could find the time to meet with even three men a week, it would take about four months to meet them all in person. Once.

I immediately set up a file system so I could keep track of all correspondence between myself and these men; without strict organization, confusion and embarrassment could occur. I had a folder for each man and I printed all e-mails to and from them, put them in the folders and prioritized them according to my interest and order that I'd respond back. Actually, after writing about two dozen of the men, I ended up taking my ad off the sites and e-mailing most of the rest of them to thank them for writing and to tell them that I just couldn't handle the avalanche of responses. It was too much, even for someone with my organizational skills.

Multiple dating was not something I had experienced in my life, nor did I want to. My typical pattern when I met someone I liked, was to see only him until the relationship ran its course. Initially, I tried to stick to this plan. The fourth man I met asked me to be exclusive on our third date and I eagerly said yes. Our relationship only lasted a few months, when major sources of incompatibility came to light. I thought about writing some of the men who expressed interest previously, but two months seemed like a long time between their interest and my response, so instead, I placed my ad again.

I had a healthy response this time, but a more manageable one. In the first week I heard from several dozen men and then it slowed to one or two every week or so. I met men for lunch at Mexican restaurants, dinner at French restaurants, coffee at Starbucks and even dated two or three of them long enough to exchange a good night kiss. They were all nice but the necessary spark remained elusive.

"It's a numbers game," Raiden reassured me during my weekly manicure. "It'll work if you give it enough time. At least now you're seeing men you like and going out to dinner, to movies, to the theatre." I couldn't argue with that. Still, I wasn't crazy about the early stages of dating and its stresses. I longed for the comfort of an established relationship although I knew that it takes time to get there and dating is a necessary step.

One day I was cleaning up my office and I ran across a response to my first ad that I hadn't tossed. His name was Larry and he described himself as a 46-year-old, 6 foot 4 inch tall, 200 lb professional who was folically-challenged. He, too, lived in Eden Prairie. As I read on I remembered why I hadn't responded to his ad—although separated for a year and a half, he was still in the process of finalizing his divorce. Although irreversible, it wouldn't be consummated until early 2000, he said. It was now January 2000. I hesitated for a moment, and instead of following my first inclination to discard his printed e-mail in the wastepaper basket, I went with my second urge to e-mail him.

My subject line read: "I know it's been two months but…" I went on to say that I was interested in corresponding with a "fellow Eden Prairie-er," if he still was. It was 7:00 a.m., January 20, 2000 when I clicked the send icon. I didn't know it then, of course, but it was the first step toward building the kind of relationship I'd been dreaming of all my life. By 9:30 that evening he'd responded and an adventure unlike any I'd ever known had begun.

Larry and I exchanged daily e-mails sharing our backgrounds, interests and amusing anecdotes until he left on a four-day golfing trip to Mississippi on February 1. He said he'd e-mail me upon his return and when I hadn't heard from him by the 7th, I decided a woman had probably accompanied him on the trip and he'd stopped writing because he'd become exclusive with her.

I didn't e-mail Larry to check out my assumption. Although some may think it's old-fashioned, I had long ago decided that I wanted a relationship where the man was the pursuer. I was also slightly annoyed that I had "known" Larry for nearly three weeks and he hadn't yet asked to meet me in person. I decided it wasn't to be, and concentrated on men who were more attentive. Still, in spite of ourselves, our relationship had its own agenda and dying wasn't part of that.

On the 11th, an e-mail from Larry appeared in my mailbox at 6:30 a.m.:

"Haven't heard from you in a bit and thought I'd check in. Are you still interested in corresponding or have you moved on, so to speak? I just want to make sure that I didn't drop the ball or say something inappropriate. In any event, have a great day and pray for an early spring!!" Larry

My response at 9 a.m. was short and to the point:

"No you didn't say anything inappropriate. I just thought that if you were still interested, I'd hear from you on your return since your last note said you'd e me upon your return with a full report. Since I didn't hear from you, I thought you had moved on. I am also looking forward to spring!" Susan

I heard from him again at 4:14 p.m. and his e-mail corrected my incorrect assumptions and moved us forward just in the nick of time:

"No, I haven't 'moved on.' I just haven't been as attentive to my e-mail world since my return from down under! I had a perfectly marvelous time. The weather was perfect (high in the low 60's, blue sky, slight breeze), no bugs, great food (catfish, barbecue, Cajun), wonderful company (myself and 3 other guys I really enjoy the company of), and superb entertainment (casinos, Cirque du Soleil, New Orleans (Bourbon Street)). I just cannot imagine a better winter getaway (unless of course it was with a lovely, smart, funny woman, of course!). My golf game was bad but the courses were tough and the greens super slick. I didn't care, tho; I just loved being able to play at all. Speaking of golf, would you like to hit one of those golf simulators with me some time?…"

I realized much later in our relationship that my last e-mail to Larry before he left for Mississippi was instrumental in finally propelling him toward asking me for a date, although he didn't act immediately. I had told him which private golf course I had grown up playing and asked him if he'd ever played it. To a golf addict like Larry, it was too enticing to ignore. I was pleased that Larry had asked me for a date but my response the next morning was terse. If he wanted to talk, he'd have to set something up in person and soon. I was tired of our e-mail relationship. I wanted to meet him.

"Welcome home Larry. I'm glad you had such a wonderful vacation. It sounds perfect in spite of the golf scores. I haven't heard of Cirque du Soleil...tell me about it, won't you? No, I am not familiar with golf simulators and yes, I would like to try it with you. What's happening in my life? I think I'll wait and tell you in person." Susan

When I received Larry's e-mail an hour later, I was surprised to find that he had changed his mind about our first date:

"...I'd suggest that we meet for lunch or a cup of coffee or whatever before we jump into the golf simulator thing, just in case you decide that you'd rather have a root canal than go on an extended date with me (the golf thing typically lasts for 2 hours or so.) If you agree with that plan, would it be convenient for you to meet for breakfast or lunch next week (the week of 2/14)? I know I have a conflict on Monday, and Fri I'm off to New Orleans again, but think that lunch on Tues-Thurs might be okay. I'd suggest dinner, but my nights next week are a bit filled at this point..."

Luckily, it didn't fully register what Larry's busyness on Valentine's Day and every weeknight that week implied: that he was at the time actively dating a large number of women. If I had known then, I probably would have fled. I wrote back okaying any time on Thursday before 6:00 p.m.

and Larry wrote me again suggesting meeting at a restaurant at the Mall of America at 1:00 p.m. for lunch.

"If you can meet on Thursday, let me know and I'll describe myself or shoot over a pic. I look just like you'd expect an engineer turned lawyer to look: somewhat geeky with a hint of smartass attitude."

Ironically, we confirmed our first date on Valentine's Day morning, three days before we were to meet for the first time:

"…Don't shoot over a pic. I like to be surprised. A more specific description would help though. I'll wear a black skirt, red long-sleeved v-neck top. As you know, I have long, blond hair, and I'll appear to be 5'8" (due to footwear)."

He wrote back:

"Sounds great! Let's see, I'll have on a brown leather jacket and I'll be wearing a blue tie with horses and cowboys on it, and I am very tall. I'll be standing there, looking very…expectant."

We met at 1:00 p.m., February 17, 2000 at the Napa Valley Grille in our nation's largest shopping mall. Larry was sitting on the couch near the door when I arrived. When he saw me, he stood. I don't remember exactly what we said or what he had for lunch (I had the squash bisque), but I do remember the laughter and the way I felt with him—happy and comfortable. When I was getting in my car to leave after our first date, my cell phone vibrated to let me know I had a message on my home phone. I picked up the message a few minutes later. It was Larry, also in the parking lot walking back to his car, calling to tell me what a wonderful time he had and how he hadn't laughed that much in a long time.

Although the spark was there immediately, we tried not to act on it. Instant and pseudo-intimacy was something we both wanted to avoid. We took it slowly. We continued to see other people, primarily because Larry wanted it that way. He believed that multiple dating would help him learn what type of woman was most suited to him. I told him it wasn't my style but if he thought it was important that perhaps he was right so I would give it a try. I did try. One week I even found the time to see three other men besides Larry. But although we made an intellectual decision to keep our options open, our hearts were drawing us closer. One night Larry and I confessed that we couldn't stop thinking about each other even when we were on dates with other people.

The night Larry asked me to be exclusive, I had just returned from a dinner date thinking what a nice man I'd been with, but he wasn't Larry and I wouldn't be seeing him again. Larry phoned while I was out and left a message. Although it was late, I returned his call. We decided we had to see each other right away so he picked me up and I went over to his apartment and he formally (and as verbose as only an attorney can be) asked me to see him exclusively. My response was a succinct yes. It was six weeks after our first date. The next morning we both called to break dates we had made with others for the coming week.

Since that day, it has just been the two of us. Next to parenthood, our relationship journey has been the most life-altering experience I've ever had. I've learned more about real love during our relatively short time together than I did throughout my entire life. July 20, 2002 we made the ultimate commitment—marriage. I am still pinching myself. I never knew that a romantic relationship could be as joyful, intimate and just plain good as ours is. Still, that doesn't mean it's been easy. We've both experienced every possible emotion in our commitment to be  together and learn how to have a healthy relationship. We've had to learn how to *be* the right person after *finding* the right person—a perfect stranger—our perfect match.

Susan and Larry Buckley
Eden Prairie, Minnesota

Helpful Internet Terms

To make the couples' stories more understandable to those unfamiliar with the Internet, I've included a list of the most commonly used Internet terms, particularly on AOL, the Internet Service Provider of all the couples in this book:

AOL—America Online. One of the first and largest Internet Service Providers.

Buddy List—A feature of AOL that allows a subscriber to make a list of the screen names of people they want to communicate with online. This enables them to see when these people are online and to send messages to them instantly and individually, as well as, setting up chat room conversations with a number of their friends.

Chat Room—Areas where people go to "talk" (type dialogue) with others. Chat rooms are either formed by a group of people who know each other or are designated areas set up by those using an Internet Service Provider. Just a few of the hundreds of AOL's chat rooms include: Places (cities everywhere in the world from Amsterdam to Denver to Toronto), Romance (Catholic Singles, Forties Love, Big and Beautiful), Arts and Entertainment (from Author's Lounge to fan clubs for nearly every celebrity to music and movie genre sites), and Special Interests (including Astrology, Beanie Toys, Car Chat, Pets and health topics).

E-mail—A system for transmitting messages electronically between computer terminals linked by telephone lines; a computer mailbox where you can pick up messages from others and send messages at your convenience.

IM—Instant Message. A typed conversation between two or more individuals that is received faster than e-mail. All the individuals taking part in the conversation can see line after line of typed dialogue in a box on the computer screen. You can scroll up to see what was said earlier and then down to the latest message.

Internet—An electronic communications network that connects computer networks and organizational computer facilities around the world. The two largest providers are AOL and MSN.

Log On—Connecting to the Internet by typing in your user name and password.

LOL—One of the most common online acronyms. It means laugh out loud.

Online—Connected to the Internet.

Profile—Information that you provide about yourself, accessible to anyone by double clicking on your screen name when you are in a chat room or if you have IM'd them. Data that can be included in a profile include: name, sex, hometown, occupation, hobbies, favorite quote.

User Name—Synonymous with screen name. It's the name you use when online. It can be virtually anything. Many people use their first or last name with several numbers (John8342), a descriptive name (RavenHair or BlueEyes500), or simply anything (Coolboarder, ScriptedEnding).

Safety Tips

Because physical safety with a member of the opposite sex is primarily an issue for women, this list is written for them. Most of these suggestions are the same common sense precautions that are wise to follow whether meeting a man online or in the real world at a singles dance, for instance. Some are specific to the Internet. However, these tips are just guidelines. They are not meant to be rigidly adhered to. Circumstances and personal comfort levels will determine what you should do in any given situation. Trust your instincts.

- Share your last name when you feel comfortable with an Internet suitor, usually after you have met in real life. You may want to check to see if your e-mail sends out your last name with your messages.

- If you're concerned about keeping your address private, you will need to have an unpublished telephone number. Using your cell phone for contact until you have a level of trust with the individual is a good idea.

- Create an e-mail account using your screen name as your e-mail address and provide only that information that you feel comfortable having anyone know, in your profile.

- When you meet for the first time, make sure it's in a public place where you feel safe. Keep the first meeting short to facilitate a graceful, quick exit if you need it.

- Don't let your guard down for the first few dates. Don't go to his house, invite him into your house, meet him anywhere secluded or ride in his car.

- Trust and follow your instincts. Every person and situation is different.

Chapter Two

Meeting Through a Personals Ad

If the idea of a matchmaker appeals to you but putting your destiny in another's hands doesn't, then be your own matchmaker. Placing an ad on one of the many Internet personals sites gives you an element of control and enables you to attract and meet the man of your dreams.

There are many advantages to placing an ad. Writing an ad doesn't require you to be Internet savvy; just to know what you want and be able to communicate it. Your ad gets you out in front of thousands of potential suitors. Most women who have tried the online personals have had significantly better results than when they tried to meet men in traditional ways (at work or church, singles dances, dating services). Also, by placing an ad, you are "approached" by men who know something about what you're looking for and believe they meet those criteria. Finally, it's a time saver. I spent many hours at singles dances returning home, disappointed, not meeting even one man I could relate to, much less want to date. At least 50 of the 60 men who answered my ad the first two days after I placed it (at age 48 and without a photo) were men I was interested in getting to know better. You won't know if there's good chemistry until you meet face to face, but at least you're certain you're are meeting someone with potential.

This chapter on writing an ad is directed to women. While it's true that many men write ads and answering their ads is an option, I don't recommend it. My view has less to do with my traditional values and more to do with what empowers women. When you answer a man's ad, you are the one making the initial contact (i.e. pursuing) and you put yourself in the position of hoping and waiting for a response which may never come from the particular man you've chosen. When you place an ad, you are empowered. You are saying what you want, then waiting for men who are interested in you and what you want, to approach *you*. You are then choosing from a number of men who are competing for a chance to get to know you better. This feels a lot better in my opinion. However, many women have found their soul mates by answering a man's ad so if that feels right to you, do it.

Writing an Ad to Attract Who You Want

First impressions are powerful. The words you use in your ad have a tremendous effect on your image and the type of man you will attract. Writing an ad that accurately portrays who you are and what you are looking for in a relationship and a partner, is your first challenge.

A well-written ad is the most critical component for finding love through the Internet personals. Computer technology has made it possible for individuals to contact hundreds of prospective dates in a few hours, even when the search is narrowed down to a limited geographical area and age group. To be noticed and then pursued by the type of man you are interested in attracting, is your goal.

The First Step: Gathering Information

To write a successful ad requires that you know yourself and what you want. Who are you? What are your interests, your dreams? What do you have to offer another? What are you looking for in a man and a relationship?

Who are You?

Who are you? Enlist the aid of family and friends for positive one-word adjectives that describe you. Are you easygoing, adventurous, intellectual, funny, creative, ambitious? Sensitive, candid, affectionate, sophisticated? Old-fashioned, playful, quiet, enthusiastic, spiritual? Make a list and circle the four you like most about yourself.

What are Your Interests?

Write down your interests and circle four or five favorites. Add one thing you don't do now but would like to learn. A friend of mine said she wanted to learn to play golf in her ad. A windfall of 50 responses came from men who were interested in teaching and sharing their passion for golf with her. A word of warning: this technique works best when you have an authentic interest in a male-dominated area such as golf, sailing, fly fishing, wood working, computers, kayaking or mountain climbing. Honesty is crucial. When making your list, be specific and original. Almost everyone likes to go out to dinner and to the movies. Consider those things that might set your ad apart from the typical ad. Some examples:

- I love everything about the sea. Its many faces, the quaint seaports and the freedom I feel when sailing and the land is a distant dream away.

- I love storms, agates, birch trees and picnics by waterfalls.

- Keeping fit is important to me but I prefer the outdoors to the gym. I love running, biking, rollerblading and cross country skiing.

- My favorite thing to do on a hot summer night is sit on the front porch swing and stargaze.

If you want to include activities that most people enjoy, be specific. Instead of saying you love to eat out, say: "I love Sunday brunches/late-night coffee shops/ Southern Barbecue/Sushi/small-town diners/haute cuisine/burgers with the works."

Rather than simply professing your love of the outdoors, say: "I love hiking/waterfalls/canoeing/ white water rafting/ wilderness rivers/the constellations/the Blue Ridge Mountains/being surrounded by acres of wheat on a windy day/collecting sea shells."

About travel, say: "I love cross-country road trips by car/bus/train/bike; I love the Swiss Alps; I've always wanted to photograph the Galapagos Islands; I like weekend getaways to quaint B&Bs by the sea to browse in small town bookstores and antique shops."

What are Your Dreams?

Don't forget to include your dreams, for he may share these or be inspired to help you realize them. Perhaps you dream of going on an African safari, touring Ireland by bicycle, co-writing a screen play, climbing Mt. Everest, renovating a historic home, taking Japanese cooking lessons, learning to dance the Tango, or starting a community service such as meals for the homeless in your town.

Identifying Past Mistakes

It's also important to think about your past relationships and why they didn't work. For instance, did you formerly choose men who fell short of your standards because you felt comfortable in the role of fixing others even though your needs weren't being met? Or did you think you didn't deserve better? Did you make financial success a priority in choosing a mate, when what your soul really needed was a man who would listen and spend time with you? Did you choose Mel Gibson and Brad Pitt look-alikes only to find that they were more interested in themselves than in pleasing you? Are you still in the "men who are too nice are boring" mind-set? Have you set yourself up for failure by pursuing men despite their lack of interest and/or commitment? Understanding and coming to terms with issues that sabotaged your past relationships increases the chance that you will find your soul mate and a joyful, healthy relationship.

The Non-negotiables

Finally, think about your non-negotiables: characteristics, habits or even lifestyle choices that would be totally unacceptable to you. Your list might include: smoking, drinking or other drug use, dishonesty, living in a big city or living in the country, having children, not having any more children, workaholics, long-distance relationships.

Non-negotiables should be used sparingly. You want your ad on the whole to be positive and upbeat.

My ad stated: "I dislike smoking, dishonesty, passivity." Although it eliminated most men I wouldn't consider dating, I did get one response from a smoker who enjoyed a cigar "once in awhile," he said. The rest of his ad sounded great and for a second I considered responding. I'm glad I didn't. Even if we hit it off initially, the smoking would eventually have gotten in the way. I dislike it that much. Know yourself and don't compromise on the issues that are most important to you.

What Are You Looking For?

Make a list of all the qualities you are looking for in a partner and relationship. You may want your partner to be romantic, generous, a sports enthusiast, health-minded, professional, ambitious, athletic, creative, expressive, confident, generous, adventurous, to love children/cats/dogs/horses/gerbils, a classical/country/rock/rap music lover, spiritual or religious, a history buff, outdoor enthusiast, homebody, good cook, or witty. Circle your top four or five choices to use later when describing what you want in a partner.

Then, decide what kind of relationship you want. If you are reading this book you are probably looking for a long-term, committed relationship. You can qualify that if you want to by indicating that friendship first is important to you. If you want to be swept off your feet and believe in love at first sight, that's okay too. What's important is that you present yourself and your desires honestly.

One caveat: honesty doesn't mean immediately revealing your negative qualities. Always focus on the positive in your ad. No one wants to hear immediately that you are $30,000 in debt, have PMS, flunked algebra in college or have 20 parking tickets. Your negatives, as well as your strengths, will be revealed eventually if the relationship gets serious. And who knows, perhaps after several months, he'll think the fact that you can't parallel park is cute.

Step Two: Writing Your Ad

Men typically admire efficiency, so be succinct. They also are intrigued by a bit of mystery so don't tell all. Prioritizing is key when writing your ad. Include only the most important aspects of yourself and your criteria. And be honest. I can't emphasize this enough. It will help you avoid attracting the wrong type of man and save you from awkward or embarrassing moments later on. Once you know what you want to say, it's time to write your ad.

Your first sentence should sum up what you most want to reveal about yourself and the type of man and relationship you are seeking. Some examples:

- Ambitious professional with work-hard-play-hard philosophy, looking for long-term relationship with like-minded male who shares a love of golf, sailing and investment strategies.

- Country girl with old-fashioned values seeking warm-hearted marriage-minded family man who can wield a hammer and enjoys the simple things in life.

- Easygoing world traveler with sense of adventure seeks male counterpart for committed long-term relationship.

Next, briefly describe yourself physically. Include age, height, build, hair and eye color. If you have been told you look like a certain celebrity you can mention that. Be careful though, I heard a story about a man whose date was allegedly a Meg Ryan look-alike. At the restaurant where they arranged to meet, he didn't see anyone who looked even remotely like Meg Ryan. They found each other only after he approached all the women sitting alone." This didn't start their date out on a positive note. Make sure that most people agree that you do resemble the celebrity. Also, if you are confident that you really do look younger than your age and you are over 35, mentioning that may increase the number of responses to your ad. For example:

- I am 52, but am told I look a decade younger. I am 5'8" tall, average build, have long, wavy auburn hair and green eyes.

- I am a petite 30-year-old Drew Barrymore look-alike.

Then write a short paragraph describing the activities you most enjoy:

- My biggest passion is golf, with tennis a close second. My dream is to someday play golf in Scotland. I enjoy quiet evenings sharing a light picnic supper in the den while listening to classical music and later, stargazing on the patio.

- I am committed to my law practice and work long hours during the week and often on Saturday, as well. My idea of a perfect Sunday is to enjoy the sunrise along with a cup of Swiss almond coffee and the morning paper; followed several hours later by a leisurely buffet brunch and an afternoon exploring bookstores.

- I enjoy the simple things in life. A plain meal shared with someone I care about after a long day of work, holding hands, kittens and puppies, long walks, and lots of laughter.

Next write one sentence describing characteristics or habits which are not acceptable to you:

- I dislike smoking and arrogance.
- Please don't respond if a drinker or overweight.

End your ad with a sentence or two of what you are looking for in a man:

- You are attractive, well-educated, intelligent with tastes that range from the sophisticated to the simple. You are able to find beauty all around you and delight in playful exploration of all the world and relationships have to offer.

- You are a caring and compassionate man who puts God first in his life and then loved ones. You have achieved harmony, peace and balance in your life. An optimist, you see life's problems as opportunities for growth.

Step Three: Writing Your Ad Headline

Most personals ads require a headline. The importance of an engaging headline can't be emphasized enough. Your headline directly affects the number of men who will actually read your ad. You must create an image that is enticing and different from the hundreds of others out there, yet consistent with the ad that follows. Again, be positive and don't sound desperate. Some examples of what not to say: "Woman Burned by Love Trying One Last Time" or "Are You the Answer to My Prayers?" Make your ad enticing so that it generates immediate interest and a desire to know more. One way to do this is by contrasts:

- Irish Fire/Nordic Ice
- High Heels to Hiking Boots
- Sunshine Smile and Stormy Eyes

Another way is to use alliteration with three or four self-descriptive words:

- Lace, Long Locks and Laughter
- Warmth, Wit, Wonder
- Genuine Grit, Grace
- Caring, Clever, Charm

Men like challenges so using an unfamiliar word can be very effective. Some examples are Salubrious (health-minded), Clinquant (sparkles like gold), Halcyon (calm, happy), Protean (versatile). Some examples of this strategy:

- Salubrious, Substance, Sparkle

- Clinquant, Creative, Class
- Pretty, Protean, Playful

Some Sample Ads

My own ad is in my story in chapter one. Two additional examples follow:

Clinquant, Creative, Class

Ambitious entrepreneur seeks male companion to share laughter and life's adventures. I am a young-looking 45-year-old petite Italian with Winona Ryder hair and hazel eyes.

My interests include five star restaurant dining, fine wine, overseas travel, art museums, theatre and Martha Stewart entertaining. I love the ocean, long walks, gardening, storms and woodworking. I would love to learn to golf this summer.

You are a health-minded, successful professional; creative, complex, ambitious, adventurous; a person of character and passion who is living "their" good life.

Irish Fire and Nordic Ice

Active, young 48-year-old Scandinavian with a touch of hot Irish blood looking for a long-term relationship, beginning with friendship.

I have a generous spirit, a warm heart and believe in living each day as though it was my last. I am easy (to talk to) and fast (to laughter). My taste in movies, books and music covers a broad range: from high drama to horror; romance to science fiction; classical to popular. I love to travel and visiting Ireland last fall was a highlight. I have a wide variety of interests including theatre, bicycling, canoeing, horseback riding, and walking. I would love to learn to sail.

I am looking for a non-smoker and light or non-drinker who is outgoing, relaxed, considerate, optimistic, honest and a good communicator.

Rewrites Aren't Just for Professionals

After writing your ad, read it to a close friend who will be blunt. Check your ad not only for typos and grammar, but content. Discuss whether your ad accurately portrays who you are and what you want. Is it positive? Appealing? When it's as polished as you can make it, it's time to move on to the next step: deciding whether or not to include a photo.

Posting a Photo: Pros and Cons

Whether or not to post a photo is a personal decision. I chose not to post a photo because I didn't want a man who would choose (or not) to respond to me based on my physical appearance. In addition, I don't think photos are a good or accurate representation of what a person looks like or if there will be chemistry. Some people are more photogenic than others and demeanor, a sense of humor, intelligence and warmth also impact how attractive a person is. I also like a bit of mystery and thought it would be more fun to see each other for the first time on our first date.

Some people prefer to post a picture because they feel that those who answer their ad after seeing their photo will be attracted to them and that will increase the odds that there will be chemistry (rather than rejection) on the first date. For a highly attractive woman, posting a photo will probably increase the number of responses. A woman who is less attractive might not receive as many responses if she posts a photo, but she can feel confident that the ones she receives are interested in her, physical appearance and all. A few hints for those who choose to post a photo:

- Make sure it is recent. The number one complaint I hear from men is that women misrepresent their age and weight. Men feel deceived when meeting a woman if she doesn't closely resemble her photograph. It's best not to use a "glamour" shot for the same reason.

- Choose a full-length photo and dress the way you usually do. If you typically wear casual skirts and dresses, wear one in the photo. If you're usually clad in blue jeans, that's the best outfit for your photo.

- With the possible exception of a pet, make sure you're the only one in the photo.

- It's easy to post a photo on the Internet. Film processing services will put a roll of film on a CD that makes the photos easy to access and send.

Online Personals Sites

There are many sites where you can post a personals ad on the Internet. Of the men and women I've spoken to, the favorites differ, particularly in different parts of the country. I am partial to OneandOnly.com because that is where I met my soul mate. But I received the most responses and met many quality men through DigitalCityPersonals.com. Other services include: American Singles.com (good site for meeting those from abroad), JDate.com (Jewish singles), BlackSingles.com, Personals@Excite.com, Matchmaker.com, Yahoopersonals.com, Match.com and SinglesWithScruples.com.

Most sites have free trial memberships, others are free to place an ad and only those responding to ads have to pay. Some, like OneandOnly, just post your essay. Others, like Match.com, have various formats and ask specific questions, but there is normally a place for additional comments where you can put your written essay. Log on and see which one suits your tastes and needs. I recommend trying at least three to see which one works best for you.

Miscellaneous Hints

- Be honest. The truth will come out when you meet in person. Be original when filling out your questionnaire and pay close attention to grammar and spelling.

- It's easy to become overwhelmed by the volume of responses and information you'll receive. I recommend keeping an organized file system, giving each person you correspond with their own file folder. Print out every e-mail you receive from them and send to them. Keep this on file as long as you are communicating or dating. It will prove to be an invaluable record of your interactions and keep you from getting your suitors mixed up. After you've found your soul mate, it will be a precious record of your romance; your story.

- Remember that you are talking and interacting with real people who have feelings. Courtesy is never outdated. Treat online suitors as you'd like to be treated. If you are not interested, rather than ignoring them, take the time to write a brief e-mail. Something like: "Thank you for your interest but I don't feel we'd be a good match. Best of luck in your search."

- Unless you are looking for a long term pen pal romance, decide how long you want to communicate on the Internet before meeting in person, and stick to it. If the two of you can't make arrangements to meet by then, move on.

Couples Who Were Their Own Matchmakers

Like the author, many couples choose to be their own matchmaker. Some like controlling their own destiny, others like the money saved by not using a typical dating service; still others like the convenience. The stories of the three following couples are vastly different but all began the same way: when one of them decided to actively seek out love by placing an Internet ad.

Sandi and Les Landers
An Internet Fairytale

An Internet Fairytale

Sandi and Les's Story

"Whatever our souls are made of, his and mine are the same."

—Catherine, *Wuthering Heights*

Once upon a time there was a romantic California girl who used to dream of finding a love that would fill her heart, mind and senses. Each evening as she brushed her long dark locks, she envisioned a love as passionate and consuming as that of her beloved fictional literary characters—Heathcliff and Catherine—lovers in Emily Bronte's legendary *Wuthering Heights*. "Whatever our souls are made of, his and mine are the same." The young girl would whisper this favorite passage to herself frequently. It was a consoling thought, although a not-yet-realized promise.

This earnest girl did more than dream. She prayed to find someone special with whom to share her life. She kissed a lot of toads, but alas, no prince emerged. She even placed a personals ad on the Internet, hoping to meet her prince there. Instead, she met even more toads: men unworthy of her affection, loyalty and good breeding.

Although she continued to dream and pray, the months passed by with the same result: toads masquerading as princes, rather than the other way around. The young girl began to lose hope. Perhaps no such man existed, at least not on the Internet, she concluded.

It was January—the start of a new year—but it held no promise of new love, she feared. The girl was distraught but resolute. She had waited long enough. She went online one last time to delete her ad.

Amongst all the replies, was one from an Englishman who was in California for a brief visit. "Could he be her Prince Charming, her Heathcliff?" she wondered. The faintest flutter of hope stirred within her. The man in the photograph resembled Pierce Brosnan rather than Heathcliff, but she decided she could live with that.

She responded to his e-mail and he wrote back. Logging on and hearing "You've Got Mail" became the highlight of her day; filling her heart, mind and senses with their growing love. She discovered he was charming, intelligent, sensitive and best of all, *Wuthering Heights* was his favorite book.

The two met briefly in person in Malibu before he returned to England. After their real life meeting, their subsequent separation and long distance e-mail relationship confirmed what they knew in their hearts when they first connected online and met in person: that they couldn't live without each other.

By February they were madly in love. He asked her to marry him in March. She accepted. He then formally asked her father for her hand in marriage. Her father gave his permission.

After drawing his sword and defeating immigration, her love arrived in California permanently in June. They were married on Maui in August. A honeymoon in England followed.

Sandi and Les's life story has the romance of *Wuthering Heights* without the tragedy. This time, Heathcliff and Catherine become transatlantic and alternate their time between the moors of England and Malibu on their journey to living happily ever after.

The moral: Fairy tales really can come true.

Sandi and Les Landers
La Crescenta, California

Mandy and Scott Maxwell
God's Perfect Match (.com)

God's Perfect Match (.com)

Mandy and Scott's Story

"Open up your Bible and no matter where it opens God will have an answer for you."

—Scott Maxwell

Still hurting after breaking up with my boyfriend of five years a month earlier, I was on the Internet to check my mail and saw an advertisement for Match.com. This Internet dating service was offering a trial month free to "meet the man of your dreams." I was only 23, too young to become a love cynic. I decided to give Match.com a try and vowed if I did-n't meet anyone by the end of the free month, I would give up my search for the man who was meant for me and just let God do his thing in my life. I overlooked one important truth: God is everywhere and does his thing, even on the Internet.

I had met only one other guy on Match.com before Scott. He was vague about details of his life and we never really clicked although I spent nearly half of my free month talking to him. After writing him a goodbye letter, I looked through my matches and saw a guy who seemed to have a great sense of humor.

When I read Scott's profile, I had to laugh. When asked what he'd like in a partner, he put he'd like someone who was 1'–5"7" tall under the height category. He had his photo posted and I thought he was cute as a chipmunk. According to Match.com's evaluation of our answers to their questions, we were 58 percent compatible. I made the first move and sent him an e-mail. By the time Scott responded, it was almost time for my membership to expire. I asked him to use my personal e-mail address instead of going through Match.com.

Scott had a practical and interesting approach to Internet courtship. His first e-mail asked what I thought were some odd questions. He wanted me to write three adjectives for each of the following: my favorite color, animal, water, and how I would feel if I was trapped in a white room. I responded: green—lush and natural; elephant—large, intelligent and sweet; water—clean, fresh and cool; white room—relaxed, calm and peaceful. Apparently he liked my answers. Scott later explained that the color is how you think of yourself, the animal how others think of you, water is what you think of sex and the white room, how you view death.

Many people think it's unwise to tell too much too soon in a new relationship. I don't agree. I didn't want to explain my history, health, family, previous partners and needs later in a relationship when it would be harder to let go if either of us couldn't accept or get past certain issues. I told Scott everything about myself including that I was having a hard time letting go of my ex-boyfriend's sons. I had known them since they were two and three-years-old; they were now seven and eight. I was still seeing them at their school and sometimes taking care of them after school. I was also honest about my appearance. I am a slightly overweight redhead and didn't want him imagining some tiny little thing.

All of Scott's e-mails were beautiful. Some even made me cry. Still struggling with my decision of how to handle my relationship with my ex-boyfriend's sons, I asked Scott how I'd know what was the right thing to do. "Open up your Bible and no matter where it opens God will have an answer for you," Scott advised. That's when I knew I just had to meet this guy. I had recently started going to church and wanted someone who would support me and strengthen my relationship with God.

I felt peace after being led to let go of the boys. One day after school I hugged them, told them I loved them but that I wasn't going to see them anymore, and to be good boys like I knew they were. That was that. No regrets, dreaming about the past and wondering what might have been. I turned my eyes and heart to the future; to Scott.

One night when we were IMing, I told Scott I had to talk to him. He called me but suddenly we were both so nervous we couldn't think of anything to say. We hung up and got back on the Internet and IM'd some more. I decided to try a phone conversation again so I called him and we talked a little longer. I told him I had to meet him and see if the chemistry was there in person. I was falling head over heels for this guy!

We decided to meet in Spokane on February 1, 2000. I lived an hour north and Scott was staying an hour east of Spokane with a friend. A 30-year-old computer programmer, he lived in Idaho and was in Washington taking some computer classes. We agreed to meet at an Indian restaurant that he loved, a place I'd never been. Just to be on the safe side, I made arrangements with a friend to meet her two hours later in case I was wrong about Scott. I wasn't.

After a buffet lunch that included Tandoori chicken, salad and rice pudding, we went to the local mall, walked and talked and Scott bought brown leather hiking shoes. He just loved the way he felt walking in them. We sat on a bench and talked about how similar our previous relationships were and how we missed the kids we had grown to love so much.

We also asked the typical date questions. One of them—"What is your all time favorite movie?"—turned out to be significant. Scott's answer was *Dark Crystal.* I watched it endlessly as a child and my dad and I would imitate the characters. My dad has been missing since May 28, 1999 in an airplane accident and it turns out that Scott and my dad are so much alike that it just blows me away. My dad used to call me Magdalana instead of Mandy, my given name. Scott had been calling me Mandaley without knowing what my dad had called me. They both make up nonsensical songs about silly things and both have given me security and love. I am positive that my dad would have approved of Scott and would have called him Scotty with an Irish brogue.

On our second date, we met each other's parents. On our third date it was Valentine's weekend and Scott agreed to help me babysit for a friend of mine. I cooked him dinner and he brought the gifts. He came armed with a dozen red roses, a cute teddy bear, pretty candle and gorgeous blue sapphire and diamond ring. I asked him what it was supposed to mean and he said that it was just a "little something" (remember that!).

Several months went by and we continued to have a great time. Scott was always so giving, sweet and fun to be with. We even kept our Internet relationship alive with frequent IMing since we both have weird sleep schedules and would talk until early in the morning when we couldn't sleep.

One day a friend of mine and I were out shopping and I found the perfect dress to get married in. It was the only white one and it fit perfectly. I had to have it. Later, I showed it to my mom and grandpa and my mom said I should ask Scott if he wanted to get married on July 1 since there was going to be a family reunion and we could combine the two. That night I called Scott and asked what he was doing on July 1 and he said he wasn't doing anything. "Do you want to get married?" I asked.

"I have to think about that one," he told me gently.

I let it go and we talked about our days. I told him I had been out shopping and had gotten some very pretty things. One day, not long after that conversation, we were walking in downtown Spokane and I saw a bridal shop and said, "Oh, let's look at wedding dresses."

"You don't need to do that," Scott said.

"Are you saying I'm never going to get married?"

"You know why you don't have to look at them," he teased me.

I wasn't going to admit anything and responded, "I don't know what you're talking about." That was that.

In June I bought Scott the Dead Ringer Harmony Kingdom box for his collection. A few days later we were out to dinner and he said that he had been looking at the box and noticed something was wrong with it. When we went back to his place I went to look at it and when I picked it up it jingled. I opened it and inside was a gorgeous diamond ring. I didn't take it out. I just closed the lid and brought the box to Scott.

"There's nothing wrong with this box," I told him.

"Yes there is; look in it."

When I refused, Scott opened the box, took out the diamond, removed the sapphire and diamond ring from my finger and replaced it with the new ring. "What is this supposed to mean?" I asked.

"What do you think it means?"

I answered his question with another of my own. "Is it a little something?"

His reply was an emphatic, "No, you know what it is."

I wasn't about to let him off the hook so easy. "No I don't know what it is," I insisted.

"Will you?" Scott asked.

"Will I what?

"You know," he responded.

It was time to be blunt. "I want you to ask; no one has ever asked me before."

Finally Scott asked, "Will you marry me?" and I said, "Yes." That was June 24, 2000 and on August 31 we were married surrounded by our parents, grandmas and closest friends; 12 of us in all. I wore the wedding dress I bought on faith before either of us proposed.

Now, Scott and I talk about how it seems that we have been happily married forever, yet feel like we just started dating. It's hard to believe that when we met we had just come out of bad relationships. We are so happy and I know my dad would be very proud of who I married and how he takes such great care of me; proud and happy that I followed God's direction and timing as he led me to my perfect match.

Scott and Mandy Maxwell
Hayden, Idaho

The Tanner family at David's graduation
Two-Stepping to Love

Two-Stepping to Love

Michelle and David's Story

"David spun me around the floor and my feet didn't touch the ground."

—Michelle Tanner

Internet dating services are like anything else in life; sometimes you have to trudge through a little mud before you get to solid ground. In my case, it turned out to be a small price to pay for the lifetime of happiness I found.

It was November 2000, eighteen months after my divorce, when I joined Nicecatch.com. My user name was Moosh and my ad headline read: Looking for a Country Boy. My ad was light and upbeat, but in truth, I placed the ad with low expectations. That turned out to be a good thing because my first few dating experiences were disastrous. One guy thought he was Mr. Wonderful but was really rude and obnoxious. Several others I met were not truthful with me about many things they told me about themselves. Disgusted, I was just about to cancel my membership when I received an e-mail response to my ad that began: "Hi Moosh, I'm David from Belton."

At the time, I lived in Independence, Missouri, about 10 miles out of Kansas City and 30 miles from Belton. I read David's e-mail. He said my ad made him laugh and he liked what I said: that I was looking for someone who liked kids, was faithful, honest, funny, loved to laugh and have a good time. He also said he liked my picture and that he was a man of his word and would treat me like a lady. That really got me going. He sounded genuine and sincere and when I saw his photo his incredible blue eyes drew me in even further.

Although I didn't know it at the time, David also had a negative experience with Nicecatch. The women he met before me were disappointing to say the least. One woman was married, two lived too far away and one lied completely about herself. Like me, Dave was new to Internet dating. He placed his ad in November too, about a year following his divorce. As a result of our similar experiences, we were both a little wary by the time we met online.

I didn't answer David's e-mail right away. I actually lost his first e-mail and then I had to go out of town to visit my family in New York. Knowing what I do now, I'm surprised I ever heard from him again. David later told me that he never really expected me to answer his e-mail because I said I liked tall, athletic, blonde men and he is 5 feet 5 inches tall. But despite my delay in responding and my height preference, when I got back from New York, there was another e-mail from David, asking why I didn't reply. There was also a voice in the back of my mind that told me to answer him; that if I didn't, I'd be genuinely sorry.

David was athletic with blonde hair and blue eyes and it turned out we had a lot in common. We were both single parents, worked out at the gym regularly, were runners, and played softball and basketball. He told me he had custody of his three kids and worked at Aventis Pharmaceuticals in Kansas City as a traffic representative in billing and shipping. He added that he was in the National Guard and would take a leave of absence from Aventis to participate in the Engineer Officers Basic Course at Fort Leonardwood from March 24, 2001 to July 24, 2001. He also said that he loved to dance and knew how to two-step, kind of.

I listened to my inner voice and answered David's e-mail just before Thanksgiving, apologizing for not getting back to him sooner. I told him I was working for the Federal Protective Service in Kansas City, was 5 feet 6 inches tall with brown hair and hazel green eyes, 125 pounds and in good physical condition from running and body building. I warned him that I could be extremely ornery, had a strange sense of humor and loved to dance. I assured him that it was okay if he couldn't dance well since I couldn't either.

We began e-mailing back and forth at least two to three times a day. By early December, David gave me his phone number and I called and left a message. When he called me back, we talked for over an hour and then began talking on the phone every day until the day we arranged to meet: December 9. David wanted to take me out two-stepping and to dinner in Kansas City after his National Guard duty.

I dropped my son off at the babysitter's house before returning to my apartment to meet Dave and when he came around the corner, took my hand, and an electric shock ran through me from head to toe. I had never had this feeling with anyone else before, even my first husband. I was moonstruck. I knew in an instant that I had found the person I was searching for my entire life.

I also had some tangible proof that David was pretty wonderful. My ex-husband was in town from New York to visit our son, and David also felt sorry for him and agreed to take him along on our first date!

In spite of the unusual circumstances, it was the best night of my life. David spun me around he dance floor and my feet didn't touch the ground. We slow danced to *Amazed* by Lonestar. David told me later that he was going to kiss me then until my ex-husband cut in. David and I danced all night long, like a scene from an old movie. When he dropped me off that night and gave me a good night kiss, I didn't want the night to end.

David called me the next day and we talked for two hours on the phone, making plans for the following weekend. He told me that he couldn't stop thinking about me and wanted to see me badly. I couldn't stop thinking about him either and was missing him already.

Our next date was even better. David took me to dinner and out dancing again. He kissed me on the dance floor during *I Am That Man* by

Brooks and Dunn, and it took my breath away. That night, he asked me to date him exclusively and of course I said yes.

Our first big challenge was having our kids meet. I have four children. My son Jared, who lived with me, was seven then. Nine and 10-year-old daughters Elizabeth and Jessica and 15-year-old Chris were living in New York with their dad so they could stay in school with their friends. David had three children from his previous marriage: Katie, 8, Ken, 11, and Mandy, 13, when we met. We knew that if it were going to work, then the kids would have to get along. Unbelievably, that turned out to be no problem. His kids adored me, I adored them and they adored my son. We saw this as another sign that our relationship was meant to be.

We spent Christmas and New Year's as a family. It was simple but incredible because we were all together. We spent Christmas Eve at my apartment enjoying warmth of the cozy fire and the magic of our decorated Christmas tree. We rented videos and had pizza. I fell asleep on Dave's chest in the middle of *The Patriot* with the cat curled up next to us. David had to wake me up after the movie and put me to bed. On Christmas day we went to David's brother Ken's house and I met him and his two sisters for the first time. We spent New Year's Eve at Dave's house watching the ball drop on television. New Year's Day we went to Ken's to celebrate his birthday and took the kids ice skating at Crown Center in downtown Kansas City. It was a very special holiday season for all of us.

In February, David asked me to move in with him while he was in school. He said that he wanted Jared and me with him and the kids permanently. I was floored and didn't know what to say. I thought about it but it didn't take me long to say yes. He was going to be away for four months in Southeast Missouri at training and he would be home only on the weekends so I wanted to be with him as much as possible. It was a special Valentine's Day. I moved in on February 14 and Dave told me that when his training was finished in July, he wanted to rent a bigger house for all of us because he planned on us being together forever. I cried. I just couldn't believe that this man could want me like that.

David and I both come from two failed marriages each so we were cautious. Although we knew we wanted to be together forever, we agreed that "I love you" were strong words and decided not to say them to each other until the time was right. I also told him that he would have to be the first one to say them. The first time David told me he loved me was in early February in front of his parents' home as we were leaving. He said it softly, thinking that I didn't hear him. I did, and when we got back to his house, I asked him about it. He said that it slipped out and that he still wasn't ready to say it. I knew how he felt. I had been sure that I loved him since January, but I wasn't ready to say it either.

By the end of February we were both ready to say those words to each other and said them on the way to the gym one day to work out. On March 23, the day before he left for the engineer course, David really surprised me. "I love you and when I come home I want to marry you," he told me.

I received my engagement ring on June 29, a week after David officially proposed to me over the phone. When he came home that next weekend, he had the ring in his hand and proposed to me again in front of the kids. We got married December 29 and left for our honeymoon in Cancun Mexico January 2, 2002.

We know that our marriage is going to last. Part of our commitment to each other is to become spiritually bonded to each other. We go to church together with the kids and we pray together, which is very important. We talk, rather than yell. We laugh, we play, and we have fun together. We try to put God and family first and foremost in our lives, because we believe that is the way it's supposed to be.

I love David with all my heart and I thank God for him every single day. And yes, we still e-mail each other back and forth at least five times a day from work, and go out and two-step once in a while too.

Michelle and David Tanner
Kansas City, Missouri

Chapter Three

Meeting in Special Interest Areas

Chat Rooms, Public Boards and Game Sites

When you stop and consider the number of chat rooms, bulletin boards and game sites on the Internet, you realize that it provides as many possibilities for contact as there as stars in the galaxy. Infinite.

ISPs usually have their own sites for games, bulletin boards and chat rooms. AOL, for instance, directs users who want to play games on AOL to keywords such as Classic Cards where users learn to play various card games and chat with other players, and Card and Board which offers bridge, hearts and chess.

When I put in a search for Game Sites, I received 2,446,644 links. One of the more original was Historic Computer War Game where players fight ancient and medieval historic battles with live people across the world. There was also a link listing the top 100 game sites that included ExciteGames, Yahoo!Games, AstroBingo, and USAOPOLY.com.

My search for bulletin boards resulted in a similar response—2,007,709 links. There were bulletin boards for almost any interest:

chronic illness support boards, an international community board for those interested in other cultures and events, parenting, investing, relationship, politics, adoption, hobbies like an Internet pond society to help those who want to create pond gardens, and even a cigar board.

There was a significantly smaller response for my chat room search; only 858,333 links. Surprising. However, many of the links, including Yahoo!Chat, claimed to contain hundreds of different chat rooms. There are chat rooms for every imaginable hobby, rooms for different ages of people looking for romance, rooms where people can talk to others in specific geographic locations, and chat rooms for various support groups.

The couples in this chapter met in a variety of ways: in chat rooms, playing Slingo, and on Mplayer. They all shared an interest that drew them to a similar site. But fate determined whether they met—if they were in the same site at the same time.

Claudia and Stephen Inoue
A Whole New World

A Whole New World

Claudia and Stephen's Story

"I was 42 years old when I took the risk to be with Stephen and now I am in Santa, Fe, after starting from scratch, and I have gained everything."

—Claudia Inoue

My husband and partner, Stephen, and I met on the Internet. Neither of us had ads posted on a personals site; we were both just surfing the net and ended up in the same chat room. Who could have guessed that a stranger living 750 miles away in Santa Fe, New Mexico would end up being the inspiration and guide for my life metamorphosis, and my soul mate.

I was living in Copperas Cove, Texas, a town of 25,000, with my two cats, Stanley and Lucy. Separated after 19 years as a housewife in a marriage without growth or passion, I was bored, stifled, and felt like my life was wasting away. Then I got a computer and discovered the Internet and Chat in the spring of 1999.

The night Stephen and I first met in the chat room on June 6, he sent me an invitation to a private chat and we chatted for nearly six hours. One of the things I shared was financial concerns—that I needed to find a job, and a reliable car. A few days later, Stephen sent me an e-mail to tell me that he'd like to give me a used car with no strings attached. I was stunned at the offer and declined, but my heart was already in trouble then.

Stephen had lived in Santa Fe for more than 20 years. As the 1999 International Drag Bike Association (IDBA) World Motorcycle Pro Stock Champion, he was well-known and liked in his home town. He seemed honest, kind and sincere. Still, I was scared and cautious. It took me several weeks just to give him my phone number and nearly four months to agree to meet him in person. After we began talking on the telephone, as well as the Internet, our connection became undeniable. We made plans to meet in person halfway between our homes.

On September 29, 1999, I found myself driving 350 miles to Lubbock, Texas to meet a man I had known for 16 weeks and three days only through telephone conversations and the Internet. I had never in my life driven that far a distance by myself; it was a huge step just to find the courage to drive that far alone. I was literally following my heart in spite of my fears, perhaps for the first time ever.

I arrived at 3:00 p.m., five hours before we were to meet. I checked into my room at the Super 8 Motel and fell asleep out of sheer emotional exhaustion. The next thing I knew, there was a knock at the door. My heart was at the door before my body made it there.

I opened the door and there was Stephen all dressed in black from head to toe with a smile that would melt all the ice at the North Pole. I reached out and pulled him to me. We hugged and hugged. His first words were, "You are even more beautiful than your pictures."

The son of a Japanese father and an American mother, I thought he was the most beautiful person I had ever seen. He makes my heart smile every time I look at him. It was love at first sight for both of us; we knew we had found our soul mate.

We spent four enchanted days and nights camping at Caprock Canyon Park: hiking, hugging, and talking, talking, talking. My heart hurt when we both headed back to our homes; it was so painful that we talked on the phone constantly and only lasted six days apart. Then once again I got on the road, 750 miles this time, to join Stephen in Santa Fe. I was spreading my wings and flying, feeling free at last.

About a month later, on October 21, I joined Stephen on a trip to Memphis, Tennessee as part of his motorcycle pit crew for the IDBA World Finals. The new world that was opening for me broadened even more.

The first time I watched Stephen go down the track at lightening speed, my heart stopped. I knew he rode motorcycles, but he was sitting on a rocket. I was excited beyond words. This immaculately dressed and manicured woman easily made the transition to blue jeans and leather. I loved my assigned duties as Stephen's official "Pit Tootsie," the roar of the engines, the smell of the burn out, and the pride and excitement I felt watching Stephen compete.

The best part of the weekend was learning more about Stephen. I heard the most wonderful things about him from the people in Memphis: his accomplishments, his character and his commitment to this sport. I now respected and admired him even more.

Two days after returning from Memphis and just one month after our real life meeting, Stephen and I went to Fort Hood, packed my belongings and moved into our first apartment on November 1. Less than a year later, I quit my job and we bought the Toyota auto repair shop where he worked. On March 30, 2001 we bought our first house together. Nearly a year later, Stephen proposed. We were married May 25, 2002 in a small, simple ceremony in the Santa Fe National Forest at Hyde State Park.

Stephen and I are a true love story. Although we work long hours together at Toy Auto Man and spend nearly all of our non-working hours together, we never tire of being with each other.

I love telling our story and encouraging people not to give up and settle for dead and unhappy relationships. Get out of them! Life is too short to stay with someone who doesn't put a smile on your face every time you look at them. I was 42 years old when I took the risk to be with Stephen and I am now in Santa Fe, after having started from scratch, and have gained everything.

Stephen and I both took a huge gamble, but it is working. A chance meeting in an open chat room on somewhere as vast as the Internet, and our immediate and continued bond has us convinced that this was meant to be. Take a risk. True love is out there. If it is meant to happen, it will. Who knows, it may open up a whole new world.

Claudia and Stephen Inoue
Santa Fe, New Mexico

Victoria and Michael McFadden
From Slingo to "I Do"

From Slingo to "I Do"

Victoria and Michael's Story

"We marvel at the serendipity."

—Victoria McFadden

I never thought the Internet games I enjoyed so much would provide more than an amusing diversion. Boy was I was wrong. They brought me my soul mate, now husband, Michael, the very first time he wandered onto a game site. We marvel at the serendipity: how his curiosity about a new game changed both of our lives forever.

I was playing Slingo on America Online (AOL) when we met. Slingo is a game that's a cross between slot machines and bingo. As you try to fill a bingo card with matching pictures from the slot machine, you can chat at the same time with anyone playing the game anywhere in the country.

I was chatting with someone about going to cooking school and Mike jumped in saying something about not going to Johnson & Wales. I was just finishing up there, so I asked him why. It turns out we were both going to J& W! It turns out that his experience at the Rhode Island campus was not as positive as mine on the Virginia campus.

It was early evening, after a long day for both of us but we ended up chatting for six hours. We had a lot more than a cooking school in common so I put Mike on my buddy list. The next day after work, we chatted online for another four hours. We exchanged pictures and continued to talk daily thanks to his sister's Web TV and the telephone, during his computer's frequent break downs.

Nearly five months later, Mike and I finally met in person the Tuesday before Thanksgiving. He traveled 682 miles and 12 hours by train, just to meet the woman he'd been chatting and phoning all that time.

At 6:00 p.m. I was pacing up and down the platform at the Newport News, Virginia Amtrak station. Several times the station attendant asked me if I was okay. I was nervous! My future might be on that train and the silly thing was late!

Finally the train pulled in and I was caught in the rush of people coming off the train. Where is he? Will he recognize me? Will he like what he sees? Will I? A million thoughts were racing through my mind.

Finally I caught sight of Mike over the crowd. He is 6 foot 2 inches and I am 5 foot 2 inches so I had the advantage of seeing him before he could spot me. I watched him approach, scanning the crowd and knew that he, too, was nervous when I heard him holler, "Make a hole or I'll make one through ya." He got through the crowd.

Our eyes met and corny as it sounds, the whole world disappeared. It was love at first sight for both of us. In the midst of all the travelers at the train station, our first kiss was better than any they show in those romantic old black and white movies.

We went to my house so Mike could meet my mom and children, then to dinner and a walk on the beach to look at the stars. He was wearing a jacket and holding me in his arms and he was shivering. I had never made a man shiver before. It was an exciting feeling.

Mike was only supposed to stay one week but he ended up staying two. We were both torn up when he got back on that train. He later told me he almost got off, but he had things to take care of back home in Rhode Island. He came back to Virginia for good January 4, 1999. I met him at the train station but this time I wasn't nervous. I was relieved that he was finally back in my arms where he belonged.

We were married December 31, 1999 at the stroke of midnight to be joined for the next millennium and beyond. Every time he kisses me I feel the same thrill I felt that first time at the train station. For a girl from Hampton, Virginia to meet a man from Central Falls, Rhode Island was pure chance. For it to work out so well is a miracle. For it to last is going to take work, love and laughter. We have all three, in spades!

Michael and Victoria McFadden
Midlothian, Virginia

Marsha Artrip and Michael Harris
Following Love

Following Love

Marsha and Michael's Story

"Money won't buy me the happiness I have found with you and I'm not going to let you slip away."

—Michael

There are many adages about love. The saying that love comes when you least expect it or aren't looking for it, was true for my husband and me. Although love's truths may be timeless, finding that special someone the way I did couldn't have happened several decades ago. When Michael and I first met, it was on our computer screens.

Divorced for three years and a 36-year-old mother of three—two girls 12 and 16 and a son, 9—the last thing on my mind was finding a husband. I wasn't even dating. Michael had sole custody of his seven and eight-year-old daughters and wasn't dating either. We both spent what little spare time we had, making friends online.

Late one night in March of 2000, we both ended up on Mplayer, a service where you can hear and even see people as you talk to them if they have a camera on their PCs. Michael had a camera, but I didn't. We could hear each other talking, as well as, the other people who were in the chat room with us and everyone took turns getting on their camera. When it became Michael's turn to get up on cam, I saw his picture come across my screen and he smiled.

That was it for me. He had the most gorgeous dimples and such beautiful eyes. I didn't speak for awhile and someone asked if MsCantBeWrong36 was "still with us." I said, "Yes, I'm still here, enjoying what I'm looking at on the screen."

Someone in the room asked if anyone else wanted to get on cam and I said, "No, I want to keep looking at "BlueEyesBoo." Michael stayed on cam and we started talking. He asked me to e-mail him a picture of myself. When he received it, his eyes opened wider and he smiled broadly. In a whole virtual room full of people he said, "You are the most beautiful woman I've ever seen."

We talked until 6:00 a.m. that first time. Over the next two weeks we talked every night online, and e-mailed each other a lot too. Then Michael asked for my phone number. The first time we talked on the phone, we discussed my relationship with my ex-husband and why we divorced, in detail. Michael said he couldn't believe that a person could go through something so traumatizing in a marriage, then proceeded to tell me how he treats a woman in a relationship. He said all the things that I, and most women I suppose, long for: to be told and shown daily that I was loved, cherished, respected and protected. We talked daily for a month on the telephone and online before Michael asked me to meet him in person. When he did, I was more than ready.

I drove two and a half hours from West Salem, Ohio on a Friday night in April to meet at the restaurant Michael managed in Toledo, Ohio. I arrived at 9:00 p.m. and I stayed until after he closed and we talked until 7:00 a.m. When Michael finally kissed me, he pulled me closer to him and squeezed me tight, gently putting his hands around the back of my neck. I had never been kissed that way. I knew then that I wanted us to become serious. When I drove back home that morning, we hadn't been apart 30 minutes when Michael called my cell phone just to tell me what a good time he had and that he wanted to see me again.

We agreed to try to meet once a week, thinking with our hearts instead of our heads. Logic told us it was crazy to begin a relationship because I was in the process of relocating to North Carolina once employment in home health care came through for me. I had friends there and wanted to distance myself and my children from my parents and ex-husband to get a fresh start where I could be my own person.

In spite of our misgivings, Michael and I went with our hearts and continued to see each other. One morning on the phone Michael told me that he thought he was falling in love with me. I felt the same way about him, but was afraid to tell him or even admit it to myself. I never thought I would find love again after such a nasty divorce.

In mid-April I went to Raleigh for an interview and Michael visited his brothers and sister in his hometown of Nightdale, North Carolina. When we both returned to Ohio, I told Michael I had been hired and would start in June. Two weeks later, I returned to Raleigh to look for an apartment. Michael called me every hour to tell me he loved and missed me. We both cried on the phone because the time to say goodbye was near.

One week before moving day, Michael called me early in the morning and said we had to talk. He told me that he couldn't live without me and there was no way he would be able to let me go that far alone. Even though his boss offered him a $10,000 raise to stay, he turned it down. "What would you say if I told you that I am moving to North Carolina too?" he asked.

I told him he really needed to think twice about what he was doing and about his children because the money would come in handy for them. "Money won't buy me the happiness I have found with you and I'm not going to let you slip away," Michael said. He packed what he could fit into his car, leaving everything else behind, and he and his two little girls came to North Carolina with me and my children.

So there we were, nearly four months after meeting online, happier than we had ever been in our lives. My grandmother once told me a story years ago. She said, "You will have many birds fly in and out of your life, but when that perfect dove flies to your door, it will confuse you, leave you breathless, but seem oh so perfect and feel right in your heart. Follow your heart and you will find your true soul mate!"

Michael and I have found our dove in each other. At Christmas, nine months after we first met on Mplayer, Michael asked me to marry him. I said yes, of course. Modern technology brought us together but Grandma's old-fashioned wisdom shows that it doesn't matter where or how two people meet, what is important is what you do after that. I'm so glad we followed our hearts.

Marsha Artrip and Michael Harris
Raleigh, North Carolina

Karen and Dave Davis
The Runaway Bride

The Runaway Bride

Karen and Dave's Story

"On my way to Mississippi to meet Dave I got in a car accident which totaled my car and made me wonder if this was a sign not to meet him."

—Karen Davis

You can't run away from true love; if it is meant to be, love will always find a way. I know because it happened to me. I was a real life runaway bride—living proof that you can't run from love forever.

There were many lonely nights while I was going through my divorce. I found that most of my friendships built during my marriage, dissolved with its ending. One night I was sitting at home learning the ins and outs of AOL wishing I could meet some new friends. I rarely went into chat rooms, but this night, for some reason I did. I sat there watching the conversations taking place and then began reading some of the profiles of the people who were in the chat room. I ran across one from a man named Dave and decided to send him an instant message and tell him that I liked his personal quote about how important his children were to him. Before long, I heard a ping and looked up and read his reply. It was the beginning of a long conversation.

It was unbelievable how many things we had in common. We were both going through a divorce, had gone through pretty nasty divorces in the past and were not ready or interested in a serious relationship. We both had lost a parent, had children, and the military was an important part of our lives. We enjoyed country music, antiquing, and were movie buffs. As we learned more about each other's likes, dislikes, past experiences and future goals, we discovered we were more than two people with a lot in common; we were mirror images of each other in many ways.

I lived in Ohio and Dave in Mississippi, but before long we exchanged phone numbers and soon after, arranged to meet. It was October of 1996 when I drove down to Mississippi with my niece to meet Dave in person for the first time. We had just passed the Kentucky state line during 5:00 p.m. rush-hour traffic. Looking to my right, I saw a car coming into my lane and swerved to avoid it. God was with us that day as we bounced off a guard rail and spun around through four lanes of traffic, never hitting another car.

The accident totaled my car but my niece and I escaped with bumps and bruises. I wondered, though, if this was a sign not to meet Dave. I debated whether or not to continue the trip but I knew in my heart if I didn't do this now, I would never have the courage again. I called Dave from my cell phone and told him what happened and we agreed that I would get a rental car and drive to Nashville where he would meet me the next day.

Early the next morning there was a knock on my hotel door and there stood Dave with flowers for my niece and me, and a look of fear and concern on his face. I was quite a sight with the bruises now in full bloom. I soon realized that the way I looked didn't matter to Dave because he really cared for me. We talked for hours on end and spent the weekend touring Nashville. When we parted, we knew it would be some time before we would see each other again but vowed to stay in touch through e-mails and phone calls.

We got together again a few months later in Pensacola, Florida where I met Dave's son and daughter. Again, time passed too quickly and I returned to Ohio. As time went on, we decided that we were meant to be together so I moved to Mississippi in January 1997. We got along well together, but I had reservations because I was still haunted by my past relationships.

Because of my fears I ran back to Ohio several months later, to the security of family and friends. But that didn't last either. I was missing Dave and he was missing me. We solved the problem by his moving to Ohio. With his job, Dave was able to live anywhere and decided it would be easier on me to remain near family and friends.

Three years into our relationship in the summer of 1998, we attended a Jimmy Buffet concert at the Blossom Music Center. It rained the entire day but started clearing in the evening. Near the end of the concert I looked at Dave and he was on one knee in the muddy grass, holding a diamond ring in his hand. As he asked me to marry him, a crowd gathered around us and I didn't know what to say. I was taken by surprise and started to laugh at first, thinking it was a joke. When I realized Dave was serious, I still couldn't say yes and softly answered, "maybe." Dave put the ring on my finger anyway and the crowd assumed I said yes, and were cheering and congratulating us. I didn't want to ruin it for everyone so I didn't contradict them.

I knew I had hurt Dave and I hated doing that. Later, he told me that he could understand my fears but that he was not like the men in my past and he would prove his love was true. He said that if having a close relationship was all we could have, he would accept it, but hoped that one day I would say yes.

In my heart I knew I wanted to marry Dave. He had a heart of gold and was so sensitive, loving, understanding, supportive and devoted to making me happy and helping me through any problems or challenges that came my way. Although I could see that he was different than the men from my past, I was still too scared to take another chance.

Retired from the Navy, Dave's work, which is classified and military-related, took him away for months at a time. During one of our separations, I met a nice man at work and we went out dancing several times—just another way to run away from Dave, although I didn't realize it at the time. This man and I started having feelings for each other, which made me question whether being with Dave was what I really wanted. I broke off our "maybe" engagement, but in the next several months, found I missed Dave more than anything. Again my heart was telling me that we were meant to be together. I also knew I would have to accept his work absences and treasure the times we were together if it was to work between us. I decided that I was willing to do this, but I didn't want to marry Dave. If we weren't married, I thought it would be easier to turn around and run if things got bad.

Another year passed. Then in October 1999 we went to Virginia Beach to vacation with Dave's children. We were on the beach one afternoon when a plane started coming our way. It wasn't unusual considering there was a military base close by, until I realized that it was circling around us with a streaming banner that read: Marry Me Karen. I looked at the children and then at Dave who was again on one knee, this time in the sand holding a dolphin ring box with a beautiful diamond ring inside. "Will you marry me, Karen?" he asked, his eyes beseeching me to say yes. This time I did.

We started planning a wedding for the spring but once again, the memories of the past started invading my heart and mind, making me unable to truly commit to this man who I knew was my destiny. As our wedding day got closer, I would think about it and become shaky and couldn't breathe. I would start to panic and want to run. Eventually I did. I called off the wedding. I felt awful about continuing to hurt this man who loved me unconditionally and would go to the ends of the earth for me. I was making everyone around me crazy with my on-again, off-again actions, but I couldn't move past my fears.

Things finally changed one day when Dave was out at sea and we were e-mailing each other. He asked if I'd like to take a trip to Hawaii for a week in February of 2000. I thought it was a great idea and then he approached me with an idea he thought was even better. "Let's get married while we are there," Dave suggested. "That way you can't run away." I agreed.

We planned our entire wedding through the Internet. And why not? After all, it's how we met. While at sea, Dave made the travel and hotel reservations. I got on the computer at home and looked for information on how to be married in Hawaii. I sent e-mails to several ministers, photographers, florists and musicians who had sites. Making my plans on the Internet, I didn't feel scared at all.

On February 13, 2000, Dave and I exchanged wedding vows at sunset on Wailea Beach, Hawaii. For those of you out there still looking for love, my advice is to be careful but don't give up. Online relationships are not for everyone, but I am glad I took the chance and sent that instant message to a stranger. Because I did, I now have a husband who has been a Godsend to me. Our next big adventure is to find a house and guess where we're looking? The Internet, of course.

Karen and Dave Davis
Biloxi, Mississippi

Decker to Decker

Dawn and James' Story

"He asked me to marry him before we met."

—Dawn Decker

At 38-years-old, I had never been married and was in an AOL chat room for the first or second time when I met the man who would become my husband. My last name is Decker and that night when I logged on, there was a person with the screen name "deckeremt." I was chatting with a friend, but when I saw deckeremt pop up on the screen, I quickly ended the conversation, wondering if this Decker was a distant relative of mine.

He wasn't. His name was James and he lived in San Francisco. Although I lived in Virginia, we talked for hours. I was surprised that the distance and my having a son and a soon-to-be adopted daughter didn't scare him off. Our Internet and eventually phone conversations continued from August 1999 until October 1999, when we finally decided that we couldn't wait any longer to meet.

I had e-mailed James a picture the children and me early on, but had never seen a picture of him. When he finally sent me a picture of himself, I sat in the parking lot of Fed Ex and cried because I had fallen in love with this man and was scared that when I saw his picture, I might change my mind. I finally got up the nerve to open the envelope and to my surprise, he was as cute as he had seemed on the Internet and sounded on the phone.

After more Internet talking and falling even more in love, James asked me to marry him before we even met. I know this sounds crazy, but I told him yes, which is not like me at all. I am a teacher and very level-headed. But the more we talked, I couldn't help but love him more. I did tell him that if I met him and it didn't feel right, that I would change my mind.

I flew to San Francisco in late October and I was scared to death. I will never forget walking off that plane. James was standing there holding a single red rose, blocking the way so I couldn't have escaped him if I wanted to. We hugged and after closing my eyes and listening to his oh-so-familiar voice, I knew I couldn't live without him.

At Thanksgiving, James flew to Virginia to meet my family. At Christmas I flew to Kentucky to meet his family. By then, wedding plans were in full force. I decided our relationship was God's will because we never had to pay more than $200 for a round-trip ticket and could afford to fly back and forth at least once a month until we were married on May 28, 2000.

Our story gets better. The one thing that kept our happiness from being complete was my plans to move to San Francisco. This was going to be very difficult for me because I am so close to my family. Again, I believe that God intervened. In June, James was offered a job transfer within his company to Virginia. That is where we live now, happy as can be.

And now for the funny part. My husband's name is James T. Decker which is exactly the same name as my brother. LOL. So, I didn't have to change my last name and my children have the same last name so we are a complete family. My family adores him and his family adores me. It's amazing to me that I even met this man, and even more amazing that everything worked out. Getting married at age 38 for the first time was well worth the wait. I'm the luckiest woman around.

Dawn and James Decker
Lynchburg, Virginia

Janet and Sid Webber
I Knew I Loved You Before I Met You

I Knew I Loved You Before I Met You

Janet and Sid's Story

"We were at a local mall and the next thing I knew, Sid had bought a ring and was proposing right in the middle of the store in front of God and all the customers."

—Janet Webber

I was sitting in West Virginia in January 2000, cold and very alone. I was trying to find someone—anyone I could have a normal conversation with. I had tried the romance chat rooms several times before and always seemed to connect to some pretty strange people. Of course I had heard all the warnings from my friends to be careful about chatting online.

As I was searching I saw the message that would change my life forever: "Hi from Tampa...50-year-old male."

Since I love the sun and warm weather, I responded by telling him I was jealous. That led to a few friendly comments and then four big words appeared: "May I IM you?" I stared at the screen not knowing how to respond. As anyone who has explored the rooms, I had encountered my share of unusual experiences through the magic of instant messages. I finally decided to try it one more time and if this man from Tampa turned out to be another bad experience, my computer was going to be turned off forever.

We "talked" for the next three hours about everything imaginable and I learned more about Sid than any man I had previously known. The wild thing was that our lives seemed to mirror each other. We had so much in common it was scary. We had both come out of long-term marriages that had gone sour. I told him I dreamed of a relationship where a man would spoil and pamper me, and treat me like a lady instead of a housekeeper and sex object. Sid told me he was the man of my dreams (yeah, right). At least he was kind and did not indicate that he wanted to suck my toes.

He asked if I had a picture that I could e-mail him. I was new to the computer world and didn't have a picture, but I did have a friend with a scanner and told him I'd send him one the next day. He had a digital camera and sent me a photo of him right away to prove he didn't have two heads or weigh 1,400 pounds.

We were still chatting around midnight when four bigger words appeared: "May I call you?" Why I gave him my phone number, I'll never know. I spent the next two hours with him on the phone, repeating myself as we continued to get to know each other (I have a West Virginia accent and he had trouble understanding me). After we said good night, my dreams that night were focused 1,000 miles south of Charleston. I was praying that even half of what he told me was the truth.

The next day started my workweek. I was a weekend nuclear medical technologist who worked from 10:30 p.m. Friday straight through until noon on Sunday. Sid was a consultant who worked normal hours. This Friday was almost like any other, spent cleaning house, getting my uniforms ready for work, and playing with my children, 100-pound Newfoundland and a spoiled rotten cat. I did have one additional activity: to scan the perfect picture and e-mail it to Sid.

The next morning when I went home to feed my children and check my e-mail, there was one from Sid. I hesitated before I opened it, wondering if it would say that he had to move to Outer Mongolia or some other place that did not have computer capabilities. When I mustered enough courage to click the read icon, I read "You are beautiful and your picture stopped my breath," before I had to rush back to work. When I finally got off work on Sunday, I rushed back home and turned on my computer to find 15 new e-mails from Sid.

The next several months we spent a lot of time on the phone and computer. We started and ended each day talking to each other. Our phone bills resembled the National Debt. During this time we found our love song. A friend of mine told me about a song she thought had been written for Sid and me: *I Knew I Loved You Before I Met You* by Savage Garden. I called Sid and told him about the song and we both ran out and bought the CD. The first time I heard the words, I cried more tears than I knew were inside me.

We arranged to meet in person on March 8. The plan was for Sid to fly up in the morning and stay for four days. On the 7th he called and said there was space on a flight leaving at 2:30 p.m. and he was rushing home to pack. My heart leaped out of my body. We were going to meet in less than five hours.

Sid's plane landed about 7:30 p.m. and I was so anxious I almost got us arrested. I could see him standing by the door waiting to come in and opened it before the flight agent did. Every alarm in the place went off. When we were finally in each other's arms, I knew my future husband was holding me.

The next day we went to a local mall and the next thing I knew, Sid had bought a ring and was proposing right in the middle of the store in front of God and all the customers. When I accepted, everyone applauded. Before he left four days later we made plans for me to visit him in Tampa. Saying good bye was beyond difficult; I felt as though someone was ripping out my heart.

My trip to Tampa two weeks later was wonderful. We spent a weekend I will never forget at Disney World and we let our love blossom like a beautiful rose. I made two more trips to Florida over the next several months.

In June I quit my job, Sid flew to Charleston and we packed a Ryder truck with my possessions and I left my old life behind to start a new one with the most wonderful man in the world. To add to my joy, Sid's two children accepted me with open arms and his daughter jumped right in and helped us plan our wedding.

We were married in the Gulf of Mexico on September 1, 2000 on a sailing yacht named *Almost Heaven,* the same as West Virginia's state song. Since that day we have painted, wall-papered, fixed sprinklers, replaced faucets, I am learning to play golf and teaching him stained glass work, and we have yet to have our first argument. Our lives are so full of friendship and love that it is unreal. I only wish that all women could be this lucky.

Janet and Sid Webber
Tampa, Florida

Chapter Four

Instant Message Encounters

Intrusions or Romantic Interceptions?

Instant Messaging, commonly known as IMing in the online world, is one of the newest Internet features to provide immediate communication and feedback through typed dialogue that appears as fast as one's fingers can type a message and press the send button.

Bob von Sternberg, who researched instant messaging for his article "Where Fingers do the Talking" in the January 20, 2002 *Minneapolis Star Tribune* notes that instant messaging has been around since 1984 when some Internet bulletin boards allowed users to hold real-time conversations with each other via their modems. But the trigger for the explosion in IMing's popularity occurred in 1996 when America online unveiled its "buddy list" function. Users compile a list of screen names of friends and whenever logged on, they can see which of them are online and reachable for messaging, von Sternberg explains. Users can create their own chat rooms with their buddy lists and talk to many people at once, or initiate a private chat with just one other individual.

Instant messaging is one of the fastest growing Internet functions, according to von Sternberg's sources. The UDC technology research firm estimated that nearly 100 million computer users worldwide sent about 900 million instant messages a day in 2001. That will jump to 7 billion a day in 2004, the firm predicted.

Instant messaging is most popular with teens (PEW Internet and American Life Project survey found that 13 million of the 17 million teens using the Internet use instant messaging). Adults typically have mixed reactions. Those with typing proficiency can find it an effective way to communicate, especially in cases of long distance relationships that would incur expensive telephone bills. Others, however, feel it is an annoying intrusion. Indeed it can be. You do not have to know a person or have them on your buddy list in order to send or receive an instant message. Unless you have blocked this feature, you can be anywhere online, in a chat room or simply reading or researching a topic of interest, and a message from a stranger can suddenly appear on your computer screen, vying for your immediate attention and response. Personally I find this disconcerting and rude. Conversely, the couples whose stories are in this chapter, and many others view instant messaging as a wonderful phenomenon. It's a miracle that led them to the soul mate they would have never met a decade ago. To me it's validation of the Internet's capacity to produce love connections in a multitude of ways, ways that address the uniqueness of the individuals and each relationship.

Janine and Michael Jannicelli
Lucky in Love After All

Lucky in Love After All

Janine and Michael's Story

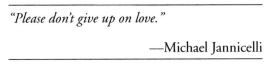

"Please don't give up on love."

—Michael Jannicelli

It was October, 1999. I had just been dumped for the second time in 23 years by my childhood sweetheart. I had left Florida to move back to my hometown of Raleigh, North Carolina, uprooting my three children to marry this guy. I was in no mood for love or relationships after finding I had been duped twice by the same man! In plain English, I had given up on men. My Internet user name was even "Not Lucky in Love."

One night while I was on the Internet, someone with the screen name "Dreamcatcher4U" came online and tried to chat with me. "A dream catcher for me—give me a break," I thought to myself. I curtly told him to get lost. In spite of my rudeness he wrote back, "Please don't give up on love. I'm sure there is someone out there for you." This time I didn't respond.

From time to time over the course of the next few weeks whenever Dreamcatcher4U would see me online, he would send me the one-line message, "I hope you'll give love another chance one day." I continued to ignore him.

He caught me off guard one day by writing more than one line. He actually wrote a five sentence paragraph. He told me that he understood how tough it was to trust again after being hurt and said that he'd pray for me. "Pray for me?!" That blew my mind. I decided to chat for awhile with this person who had now piqued my interest. His name was Michael.

Michael was nothing like the men I was typically attracted to. I had always dated high profile men with graduate degrees and high incomes. Michael was blue collar all the way. He worked in a warehouse, drove a truck and wore blue jeans every day. He even had his longish dark hair pulled back into a short ponytail. I was conservative, a business professional who always dressed fashionably.

We were from different worlds in other ways. Michael was one of six children, raised in a close-knit family with lots of noise, love, warmth, laughter and traditional values. I was an only child. My father left when I was two years old and my mother raised me alone. Family was just the two of us and we didn't have a lot of time to spend together.

Although an unlikely match, we started talking on the phone for hours at a time. After a month we met and I continued to see Michael as a platonic friend. In time I found he was unlike the men I was used to, in wonderful ways. He went to church and he prayed. He was compassionate. He would buy a homeless person a meal and help anyone who needed it, in any way he could. He was patient with my children and respected me and my values. I felt a certain quietness, simplicity and genuine kindness in Michael.

My stubbornness about maintaining strictly a platonic relationship with Michael eased a bit one day when he walked into my office wearing the one suit he owned. I was speechless. It was a beautiful suit and he looked terrific. I began to view him in a whole new way from that moment on: as a possible mate. I laughingly told him, "If you ever marry me, I want you to wear that suit."

A major snowstorm in January of 2000 was another turning point in our relationship. I had never been in a snowstorm and Michael called, then came over to help me prepare for the storm. He made sure there was enough food for me and my three kids, split a ton of firewood and showed us how to build a fire.

We were snowed in for five days. Still platonic friends, we sat up all those nights talking, listening to music and answering questions from "getting to know you" quiz books. The more I got to know Michael, the more I loved, respected and cherished his companionship. Suddenly I discovered I wanted more than friendship, and I found that he did too when we shared our first kiss on the fifth day of the storm.

From then on, we were together as a couple all the way. I already shared some of his interests, particularly fishing, hunting and camping. And Michael was open to experiencing opera, ballet and the symphony. I was surprised to find that not only did he stay awake, but truly enjoyed each event.

Michael's three children got along great with my three children. We were like one big happy family. In November of 2000 he asked me to be his wife. I couldn't say yes fast enough. We agreed that life is too short and quickly planned a wedding. We tied the knot January 5, 2001 with Michael wearing the suit that helped open my heart to him. I'm so glad Michael convinced me not to give up on love.

Janine and Michael Jannicelli
Raleigh, North Carolina

The Yankee and the Southern Belle

Colli and Ray's Story

"I would never consider dating anyone north of the Mason Dixon line, and a firefighter at that."

—Colli Bounds

I hadn't had a boyfriend since 1994, my junior year in high school. I was cute and had plenty of friends, but not a boyfriend. When I started college at the University of Tennessee at Martin in the fall of 1996, I thought all that would change.

Unfortunately, it didn't work out as I had planned. I joined a sorority and went to fraternity parties, but I could never find anyone that caught my eye. I had plenty of luck setting my friends up. A few of them are married to the person I set them up with. But I couldn't find anyone for myself. I used to cry myself to sleep every night wondering when I would find that one special person.

I even prayed and bargained with God. "God, if you will just send me someone, I promise to start going to church more and do everything that you want me to do," I pleaded. Needless to say, that one didn't work. I seriously considered joining a convent. Instead, I switched to the University of Memphis in the fall of 1997. New college, still no boyfriend.

This long-standing course of events changed with one simple act—the purchase of a computer and my introduction to the Internet. One day in

July of 1998, I was online in the Memphis chat room talking with the other regulars when I saw an unfamiliar screen name. A voice inside me was insistent. "Instant message him," it screamed. I have never believed in fate or destiny, but this time I decided to obey my inner voice.

His name was Ray. He told me he was from Fairfield, Connecticut but now lived in Memphis and was a firefighter. Raised with strong Southern values, I would never consider dating anyone north of the Mason Dixon line, and a firefighter at that. To be involved with a man having a 24-hours-on-24-hours-off schedule who put his life on the line nearly every day, and a Yankee at that, was unthinkable. Still, I decided that it wouldn't hurt to just chat with him a bit.

We continued writing back and forth for several hours and I found that we had a lot in common. We both liked the outdoors, especially hiking and camping; sports like baseball and basketball; and country music. A former law student, now pre-med, I wanted to be with a man who would stimulate me intellectually. Ray was clearly intelligent, but more important, he made me laugh. A lot.

We agreed to meet online the same time the next day. When I signed on and saw his name, I was so happy. I could hardly wait to open my mailbox and see what he had written. I don't think I stopped smiling from the moment I opened his message until after I typed and sent back my response. We continued to talk for a couple of days on the computer and then Ray did it—he asked for my phone number. I was so excited, I could hardly type.

The first thing I noticed when Ray called was that he had the thickest Yankee accent I had ever heard. He said I had the thickest Southern accent he'd ever heard. After getting over that obstacle, we talked, or rather, he made me laugh, all night long. We got along so well that we continued phone conversations for several nights, each one getting longer and longer.

A week later, Ray asked me if I wanted to meet. His brother Dave and friend Mike were in town from Connecticut to attend his graduation from the firefighter academy that Friday night. So not only would I be meeting Ray, I would be meeting his brother and best friend. In spite of the pressure, I rose to the challenge. We decided to meet at the Mapco gas station because it was a safe public place and easy to find.

When I pulled into Mapco, my heart was beating so fast I could hardly breathe. I saw three guys standing there and got out of my car and approached them cautiously. I spoke first. "Hey," I drawled.

When Ray said, "Hey," I recognized his Yankee accent at once. A clean-shaven, 6 feet tall, 170 pound man with brown hair and gorgeous sapphire blue eyes stood in front of me. It was love at first sight for me, as soon as our eyes connected (second sight really, as our personalities connected before we ever laid eyes on each other). Then everyone started talking and we decided we'd go downtown to Memphis' famous Beale Street and grab dinner at Alfred's.

I followed them in my car. While driving, I received an emergency call on my cell phone. I worked for an agency that served the mentally and physically handicapped, and one of my clients was having a seizure. The woman who was working didn't know how to handle it. When we arrived at Alfred's and I stepped out of my car, I was still on the phone talking her through the seizure.

Ray said that's the moment he fell in love with me. He was impressed that I could handle that stressful situation so calmly. When we walked down Beale Street under the Silky Sullivan's sign, he gently took my hand. My heart soared. I was already crazy about this guy before we met, but now that we had, I thought he was perfect.

At dinner, Dave and Mike revealed stories of Ray's boyhood antics and we couldn't stop laughing. Later, when Ray walked me out to my car, he leaned in and gave me the sweetest kiss of my life. It was so soft and gentle. I don't even remember driving home because I was so preoccupied with thoughts of him.

We are still together. If it weren't for the Internet, I know Ray and I would have never met. The Internet allowed what appeared from the outside an unlikely match, to germinate and grow. Innocent chatter to genuine interest to deep love in real life.

Colli Bounds and Ray Pelletier
Memphis, Tennessee

Kristen and Travis Heckel
Windows to the Soul

Windows to the Soul

Kristen and Travis' Story

"Ever since I was a young girl, I believed I'd know my husband as soon as I looked into his eyes."

—Kristen Heckel

Who would have thought that one new modem and an account with America Online could change two lives so drastically? When I look back now, I realize that with one faulty double-click of the mouse I could have deleted my chance to be with my soul mate. Ever since I was a young girl, I believed I'd know my husband as soon as I looked into his eyes. At age 25, this came true. What I never would have guessed, was how long it would be from the time we met until I looked into his eyes; a result of meeting in such a non-traditional way.

Although I had been teaching high school English in Owensboro, Kentucky for nearly two years, I was still homesick for my hometown of Louisville. I decided to use my 1998 tax-return money to upgrade my ancient computer to keep in touch with family and friends.

One week into my online experience, I had already encountered Internet users who were after more than just a nice conversation. So late one night when an instant message (IM) from a "MrTheeng" popped up on my screen, you can imagine what was going through my mind. "Another pervert," I thought. My usual response to an unsolicited IM was a swift click of the cancel button. For some reason, I didn't do that this time. Instead, I clicked on his user profile and decided he seemed harmless and would be fun to chat with, so I responded.

Despite my misgivings about meeting men on the Internet, we began to chat regularly. In a city where I felt totally isolated, MrTheeng, or Travis, made me smile and feel less lonely. When he'd get home from a night on the town, he'd e-mail me stories of his adventures. He was my link to Louisville. We also talked about our mutual love of disco music and my ardor for Gene Simmons and Ricky Martin, exchanged re-written satirical song lyrics about each other, and Travis would send caricatures he had drawn of himself and me.

Surprisingly, I was the one to move our relationship to the next level: the telephone. I was going to be in Louisville April 13 to interview for a teaching position. Typically not a forward person, I asked Travis if I could call him while I was in town. Now Travis was the hesitant one, embarrassed by his Kentucky accent, he said. Eventually, I was able to sweet talk him into letting me call and we talked and laughed for more than an hour. The chemistry was undeniable.

Travis and I began talking on the phone several times a week and exchanged photographs three weeks later. I was pleased and surprised when I downloaded a picture of a tall, blond guy standing next to a sporty blue Mustang. He was intelligent, nice, witty and good looking. Meeting someone like that on the Internet seemed too good to be true.

Travis wanted to meet in person, but I refused because I had heard crazy stories about online affairs gone bad. He finally got his way through a bet I was sure he'd lose. Travis bet me he could watch my favorite soap opera, *Guiding Light* for four weeks and send me a daily synopsis. If he succeeded, for the first week he'd win a date with me on June 27 to do one of his favorite things: watch a televised World Wrestling Federation event. He'd win a tennis game, picnic and car wash with me for the second, third and fourth weeks.

Much to my surprise, I found a daily summary of *Guiding Light* in my AOL mailbox for four weeks straight. I would be forced to pay up. I was glad I had a month to get used to the idea. Although I didn't get the job I interviewed for in April, I was going home to Louisville. The joy and excitement of moving home helped keep my fears about my relationship with Travis somewhat at bay. Fears or no fears, Travis was a constant presence in my life. We began to chat online and on the phone more frequently. Travis started chatting online with my mom as well, and she encouraged this communication so she could question his intentions.

In late May, Kentucky spring weather slapped me in the face. A storm left a fallen tree on my car; its branches piercing the convertible, cracking the front windshield and mangling the frame. I was distraught and inconsolable, or so I thought until the doorbell rang and a UPS man handed me a package from Travis. In this ordinary-looking brown box was a Gene Simmons doll and a Ricky Martin CD. His thoughtful gesture made my tragedy manageable. After my Memorial Day move, Travis sent me a Hershey's kiss made of glass he'd blown himself. That he'd go to these lengths to make me smile, both touched and scared me.

Was Travis a psycho or sincere? This was a question I asked myself and one I couldn't answer. I had other questions and fears. We enjoyed each other's conversations, but what would happen when we met? Would we be disappointed? Fulfilled? I only knew that I cherished what we had and was scared to risk it with a meeting.

The pressure to pay my debt for the lost bet was on, even though the wrestling event was not until June 27. Every day was the same: Travis asking me out and me turning him down. The only thing he wanted for his June 7th birthday was to meet me, and I still said no. With each passing day I grew more and more leery about meeting. Travis offered to let me out of our bet. Although every ounce of me was scared senseless and wanting to back out, I stood by my belief that a bet should be honored. We arranged for him to pick me up at my home at 6:30 p.m. I told Travis that

I would come out to his car. I didn't want him to meet my parents yet; it signified a commitment I wasn't ready to make.

June 27 finally arrived. While I was getting ready for our date, my parents' phone rang. It was Travis trying to convince my mother to let him come inside the house when he arrived. I was livid. Minutes later, my phone rang. Again it was Travis, this time asking for directions to my house. I lit into him for going behind my back. He offered to cancel if I was that upset but I refused, just wanting to get the date and the debt over with.

A little later the phone rang again. "Um…I just wanted to let you know that I look nothing like my picture and I hope that is OK," Travis solemnly stated. I hung up without responding as my anger flared again. I felt like a fool for believing that someone as handsome as the man in the picture he sent would be involved in this situation. Images from weirdos to circus freaks were swirling in my head. I calmed myself with the thought that these images turned out to be true, I could block him from any messages online and ignore his phone calls.

Promptly at 6:30 p.m., a blue Mustang pulled into the driveway. I took a huge breath and hesitantly left the security and anonymity of my house. The walk to the car seemed never-ending. I reached for the car door handle and closed my eyes. "Well, do I look like my picture?" a familiar voice asked.

When I opened my eyes, I discovered he did look like the picture he sent, with a few minor exceptions: a huge afro wig and a silk polyester disco-style shirt. What else could I do but burst into laughter?

"I knew you were anxious so I had to calm your nerves somehow," he explained. I was touched by his gesture. How many of us would risk the important first impression to ease another's fears? I looked into Travis' blue eyes. Seeing his sincerity and generous spirit radiating through them, I knew from that very second that I wanted him to remain in my life. I wanted to know him and be near him always. Six weeks after our first date, we were engaged.

Travis and I were married August 4, 2000. Even though our courtship was brief, Travis and I had no doubts we were meant to marry. Despite my initial fears about meeting someone on the Internet, worked our perfectly for us. It enabled us to see and fall in love with each other's souls before we ever laid eyes on each other.

Kristen and Travis Heckel
Louisville, Kentucky

Author's update: Kristen and Travis have written to tell me that they celebrated the birth of their first baby—Aiden Parker—in September of 2002.

Tammy and James Newman
Cyberspace Celestials

Cyberspace Celestials

Tammy and James's Story

"I was invited to go on a date with a man...a real live man that I could see and touch. I turned him down to go home to chat with a man that so far, wasn't even real... just words on a screen."

—Tammy Newman

Some people believe there are angels always in our midst; watching over us, guiding us. I like to take it a step further. I think we are all angels with the purpose of touching each other's lives in varying degrees; intended by God to help each other in our earthly struggles. I also believe that if we listen, we're eventually led by God to the perfect person for us; that person whose life will be intimately entwined with ours forever and bring us heaven on earth. Anyway, that's how I see what happened between J and me.

I was in the midst of breaking up with my boyfriend of more than five years in January 2001. It hurt a lot, but I put a smile on my face and kept busy, trying to enjoy life. I refused to feel sorry for myself. One night while I was online surfing around, I received an instant message from a man named James who decided to say hello after reading my profile. We chatted for a little while.

I wasn't interested in starting a serious relationship with anyone online so I kept my conversations with James casual and brief for several weeks. I was also quick to inform him that I wasn't looking for a romantic relationship; that my life was full and I didn't under any circumstances want any complicated or long distance affairs. Someone had already broken my heart, I explained, and once was enough for me.

J (my nickname for James) seemed okay with that. We both wanted the same thing—an uncomplicated, wonderful and lasting platonic friendship. He lived in New Jersey and I was in Florida. In addition, I was six years older than his 32 years, so a relationship that was strictly friendship made sense.

From the beginning, I felt lucky and happy to have a male friend like J. I liked that his first question to me wasn't, "What do you look like?" That's usually what I encountered. He was more interested in knowing where I lived, what I did for work, my hobbies and interests. I told him I'm the marketing director for our local blood bank, enjoyed scuba diving, cooking and did a lot of volunteer work for my community. His curiosity about me and my world, rather than my physical appearance, drew me to him more deeply and faster than I wanted or could have imagined.

Before I knew it, I couldn't wait to get home and log on to see if there was an e-mail from J. Oh how he could make me laugh out loud! He is by no means a comedian. He is just one of those people who embrace the light side of life. He brought true laughter out of my heart and soul and it felt so good.

After a couple of weeks of casual chatting and e-mails, J asked me for my phone number. I don't know what came over me; I have never been so quick or eager to give my number to anyone. Just like that, I gave him my number and a minute later I was able to put a voice to the words on my screen. He had the sweetest voice and a laugh that I could feel through the phone line. My heart skipped a beat the first time he said my name out loud.

We talked and laughed and shared some personal stories from our pasts, stories that revealed his good character. It didn't take long for me to realize that he was a truly warm and wonderful man, a good daddy and a wonderful son. From the way he spoke of his previous marriage and ex-wife, I knew he was a good husband, as well.

It felt so comfortable and right talking with him on the phone. We talked for hours. I couldn't get enough of him and I didn't want each conversation to end. Our instant messages, e-mails and phone conversations continued and got more intense with each passing day. We had learned so much about one another, yet every day we learned something new.

One day J shared that he had recently met two other ladies through the Internet and was disappointed both times because they stretched the truth about themselves. He swore he would never meet another online lady in person again, except for me of course, because no matter what, we would be friends forever. That took my breath away. The conversation also helped me to understand J's reaction when he saw my picture for the first time. I was on the phone with him when he opened the letter it was tucked in. He sounded shocked as he asked me, "Is that really you?" I thought he was disappointed, but he said he was used to women sending him old pictures or pictures of someone else and he just couldn't believe that it was recent and really me. As it turned out, he really liked the pictures.

Soon after that conversation I was invited to go on a date with a man…a real live man that I could see and touch. I turned him down to go home to chat with a man that so far wasn't even real . . . just words on a screen.

When I got home, there was an e-mail from J with his picture attached. My heart stopped. In that instant I knew I was in way over my head. My very first thought as I looked at the photo of a slightly balding, big-cuddly man with a goatee, beautiful twinkling blue eyes and a smile to melt my heart was, "This is the man that I am going to spend the rest of my life with." Now I was able to put a face and a smile with the words and the voice. I began to wonder about this infatuation and if it were really possible to fall in love with someone I hadn't met in person. My days were filled with daydreams and wandering thoughts of what the future might hold for us. I had completely forgotten that I didn't want anything to complicate my life.

I just couldn't let J know how I felt, though. I pretended that I still just wanted a friendship with him. That is, until an unexpected incident broke through my facade. After about three weeks of this whirlwind we had been in, I came home after a bad day at work to find an electronic card in my mailbox from J. At first it made my bad day just fade into a distant memory as I read the beautiful poem. Then tears began to fall as I read J's message that followed the poem: we couldn't instant message or e-mail much longer because he had been borrowing his mom's computer and she wanted it back.

J promised that we could keep in touch by the phone and mail but somehow I didn't think that would happen. Even if it did, I felt we were losing something valuable and special—our Internet connection. In that moment I realized what an important part of my day he had become. It scared me beyond words.

The next day I called him on my cell phone. I was supposed to be at work but I couldn't work. I just wanted to talk to J. I drove around town for hours with my sweet James on the phone: talking, crying, laughing. I went to the beach so J could hear the seagulls and the ocean. I wanted to get on a plane at that very moment and go to him. That day I told him that I was going to come to him; to be near him, to meet him.

That night I e-mailed J parts of my journal. I took the risk and revealed my most secret thoughts. I shared with him my growing feelings and desires for him. The next day he e-mailed me back and said that now that he understood how I felt and that he was going to wait and see what God had in store for us—leave the results in God's hands.

I could not believe what I had just read. I must have read it a hundred times. I felt strongly that God brought us together to be each other's guardian angels, helping each other through the hard times we were going through following our relationship breakups and other personal struggles, and bringing laughter back into our lives.

J had often touched my soul with his words: telling me he was proud of me or worried about me or that I was funny. And now he touched my soul by telling me he would put our relationship in God's hands…it was that important to him. We set a date in April when I would come to him. I counted the days and hours. As it turned out, we didn't have to wait that long.

On February 1, J told me that his heart was screaming for me. The next day I got on a plane and flew to Philadelphia to meet him. Although I was excited and eager, I was completely at ease during the flight. I was not nervous at all. I knew what I was doing was right. My plane was late and I learned later that J was so nervous that he was pacing back and forth and even ended up telling a complete stranger about us. Later when we left the airport, although he lived 20 minutes from Philly and is very familiar with the area, he was so taken with me, he got lost three times. We still laugh about that.

When I first got off the plane and walked into the busy concourse with hundreds of people milling around, there stood J with a smile that melted my heart. I know it sounds cliché, but suddenly everyone disappeared, time stopped, and the world stood still as James walked over to me and reached out and kissed me. I knew this was forever and that my life was now complete. He said it all with his kiss.

From then on, things moved along pretty quickly. J came down to Florida to check out some jobs and the area. Our original thought was that he would move down during the summer and we would plan a big wedding for the fall. But again, things didn't work out that way. On the second day J was in Florida, I took him down to the river. We were walking along the river's edge and he stopped and hugged me. The sun was shining and there was a gentle breeze blowing. "I love you," he said. I told him I loved him too. He asked, "How much?"

"To the moon and back," I said. Then he asked me when we were getting married and I told him I would marry him whenever he wanted to.

He pressed me for a specific date. "I would marry you this very minute if there were a preacher here" I said.

"Really? Now?" A look of surprise and delight crossed his face.

"Yep, and I even know someone who could perform the ceremony," I told him. Just then some bells from a nearby church began to ring. He kissed me so sweetly and said, "Let's do it!" At first I thought he was kidding, but he wasn't.

So at noon on April 12, the original day we were to meet, I called Lisa, a notary at my bank, and we went to the court house to get the marriage license, begging the judge to waive the three day waiting period. Then we went to the mall and thanks to prom season, I found a beautiful dress and shoes. J bought pants, shirt, belt, shoes and socks. Then we bought the wedding rings and picked up a simple bouquet of blue daisies, champagne and film. I called a couple of my closest friends and told them where to meet me at the river dock at 8:00 p.m., no questions asked.

By 8:30 p.m. we were husband and wife. The spot we chose was very meaningful because it was the place where J says he first realized he was falling in love with me. The funny thing was that when that happened, he was in New Jersey and I was on that Florida pier talking to him from my cell phone so he could hear the seagulls and the surf. We both had fallen in love before we met.

And now? We are living happily ever after, trying to make a baby.

James and Tammy Newman
Sebastian, Florida

Chapter Five

Other Online Oases

Limitless Paths to Love

The last four stories illustrate the endless paths to love available on the Internet. One was not an Internet meeting, yet without e-mail which the Internet provides, this couple would not be married today. The second story illustrates how posting a profile can attract your soul mate, even if neither of you is looking; just searching for the answer to a question. The third couple found love when the woman called the AOL tech support center for help with her Internet problems. Showing her parents how to do a profile search so they could find people with common interests to chat with is how the woman in the fourth story found her soul mate. If you haven't found love in the typical ways on the Internet, remember that there are ways of meeting online that haven't been covered in this book, ones that perhaps haven't yet occurred—new frontiers. You could be an Internet pioneer so be hopeful and open and you will meet your soul mate when you least expect it.

Ron and Judy Mullenax
E-mail Reunion

E-mail Reunion

Ron and Judy's Story

"I didn't even know Judy's last name but I did have her e-mail address."

—Ron Mullenax

I've heard it said that when the student is ready, a teacher will appear. Four years following my divorce, I was a man desperately in need of new life. Sadly, it was the sudden loss of my father that taught me to stop feeling sorry for myself, quit dwelling on the past, and to learn to enjoy life again. This new attitude propelled me into a chance encounter and subsequent reunion that dramatically changed my life.

It was May of 1999 and two friends asked me if I'd like to join them on a trip to Mexico. Their timing followed my epiphany, so I agreed. Since it was a 6:00 a.m. Saturday morning flight, I decided that staying up all night made more sense than going to sleep, just to awaken at 3:00 a.m. I could sleep on the flight, I reasoned. Naturally, I was very tired when I arrived at Cleveland's Hopkins International Airport, took my seat, and settled down for a three-hour nap.

Two ladies sat next to me. They were bubbly, excited and talkative. "Great," I groaned silently. "No sleep for me." Then I noticed the girl on the aisle, whose name I soon found out was Judy. As exhausted as I was, her attractiveness won over my fatigue, and we chatted the entire three hours. I wanted to see her again. Soon.

Judy was staying in Cancun for three nights and I was going to Playa Del Carmen, 45 minutes south of Cancun, for seven nights. We agreed to meet Monday at Xcaret, an ecological park a few miles from my hotel that was already part of her itinerary. However, when I arrived at the appointed time, I found no Judy. Frustrated and confused, I returned to my resort. Since they were returning to Cleveland on Tuesday, this flame of romance had been quickly extinguished. I didn't find out until later, that due to the language barrier, I had missed a message from Judy saying she wouldn't be able to meet at that location.

Although I didn't even know Judy's last name, I did have her e-mail address. During the week I wrote a quick note from an Internet Cafe in Playa and told her I was happy to have met her and was sorry we hadn't been able to hook up during our stay in Mexico. When I returned home to Ohio and checked my e-mail, sure enough, there was a message from Judy. We made arrangements to meet later that week in Fairlawn, half-way between the Cleveland suburb of North Royalton where I lived, and Judy's hometown of Akron.

Our date grew near, and plagued by fears and doubts, I decided to cancel at the last minute. I decided I really didn't have the energy to start a new relationship or courage to risk the rejection I was sure would follow. I didn't expect to hear from Judy after that and decided it was for the best.

Three months went by and one day while I was online, I saw Judy's name on my Buddy List. I decided to say hi and she responded. A caring and forgiving person, Judy agreed to once again set a date to meet for drinks. This time I showed up.

We talked for more than three hours. We decided to see each other again. And again. And again. We've enjoyed movies, gardening and biking together, but we especially love to travel. We took a cruise from Grenada to Venezuela and a trip to Tikal, Guatemala, to see the Mayan ruins.

On January 13, 2001 we took our most exciting trip ever when we traveled back to where it all began—Playa Del Carmen—and were married January 17. We exchanged our vows kneeling in front of a wedding altar deep in the jungle. Our wedding was Mexican all the way, from the Mariachi band to the traditional Mexican Three Milk wedding cake.

I guess fate does exist and I'm sure glad it had the patience to deal with me. Our Internet reunion led me to a new life, which is the happiest ever.

Ron and Judy Mullenax
Brunswick, Ohio

Paula and Anthony Birkholz
Karaoke Connection

Karaoke Connection

Paula and Anthony's story

"If you have family, friends, health and music, what more do you need?"

—Anthony Birkholz

I met the love of my life on the Internet. We did not meet in a chat room, on a message board, at a public site or through the personals. Meeting someone on the Internet or anywhere else, for that matter, didn't even occur to me. Starting a relationship was the last thing on my mind.

It all started when a girlfriend asked me to go to Austin, Texas for the weekend. We were both separated and going through a divorce and needed to get away from that stress and familiarity of our rural town of 4,000. I enjoy singing, and especially karaoke, and wanted to do that while we were there. But, where to go? Then I had a brain storm. I decided to go to the AOL member directory and find someone who lived in Austin and ask them.

I found several profiles of Austin residents, including Anthony's. I sent him an e-mail asking where to go for karaoke in Austin. His personal quote was: "If you have family, friends, health and music, what more do you need?" It really touched my heart and I told him so.

Three days later I got a response. Anthony sent me an e-mail suggesting I go to the Chelsea Street Pub and asked me what 0309 from my screen name Psmith0309 meant. I explained that it was my birthday. Amazingly, it turned out it was his birthday too.

Later that night, I was online when I received an instant message from Anthony.

We chatted, sending messages back and forth for two hours before I went to work. He told me that he was originally from New Jersey and had lived in Texas for two years. We talked about our families, music and work. He is a banker and I am a correctional officer. What a combination. Still, there was a feeling of comfort and knowing that was undeniable. We decided to talk on the phone the next night and we talked for three hours.

I never did end up going with my girlfriend on the Austin trip because my dad underwent heart by-pass surgery. Three weeks later, Anthony and I decided to meet and I drove four hours from east Texas to meet a man whom I'd never even seen a picture of.

We met at Austin's Highland Mall parking lot at 7 a.m. and immediately gave each other a big hug. I thought he was cute and very polite. We ate breakfast at the International House of Pancakes and he told me later that he couldn't stop looking at my eyes because he couldn't believe how green they were.

After breakfast, we went back to his apartment so I could rest. That might seem like risky behavior to some people, but my instincts about people are usually correct and I felt strongly that Anthony was someone I could trust. I had been awake for over 30 hours and was so tired that I went to sleep sitting on the couch. When I woke up, Anthony was holding my hand. I couldn't believe such a small gesture could mean so much. At that moment I knew that he was a sensitive and caring person. I was comfortable staying with him at his apartment, and he was kind enough to give me his bedroom and make up a bed for himself on the couch.

We did a lot of things during our first weekend together. We went to see the movie *Duets*. We had dinner with his parents, and of course, we went to karaoke. I sang *Valentine* by Martina McBride and Anthony sang

I'll Be by Edwin McCain. We also sang a duet: *Just You and I* by Eddie Rabbit and Crystal Gayle.

Anthony also told me that his sister had met someone online and had gotten married, but that he didn't think it could happen to him. Something was happening, though. In spite of the fact that I had fears about getting into a relationship before my final divorce papers were signed, and Anthony had gotten hurt in two previous relationships, our connection was growing.

Three weeks later, Anthony came to visit me and meet my family and friends at karaoke. Three more weeks passed and he invited me to his bank's Christmas party. That weekend he told me he loved me. It scared me to death. I told him that I liked him a lot and enjoyed his company but I wasn't ready to say those words to him. Little did I know that I would be ready much sooner than I thought.

On January 7 we were talking by IM after I returned from an evening of karaoke with some friends. I was telling him about the evening, how much I missed him, and that it just wasn't the same anymore without him there with me. He asked me if I ever wanted to get married again. I told him that I that I might. The next thing I knew, he sent me an e-mail at 2:22 a.m. asking, "Will you marry me?" I responded, "Yes, but you will have to ask me again in person."

We weren't able to see each other again until January 20th. This time I met his sister and her family and we joined all of his family and his co-workers at the Chelsea Street Pub for an evening of karaoke. Anthony was one of the first to turn in a song to sing, but when they called him up, he said he had something to say first and asked me to come up on the stage.

Anthony got down on one knee and said, "Paula, you know how happy you have made me and you know how much I love you. Will you marry me?" All I could do was stand there with my hands over my face. After I got over the shock, I said yes. The audience stood up, clapping and cheering.

On April 3, 2001, I got a job transfer from Skyview /Hodge Correctional Facility in Rusk to the Travis State Jail in Austin, and Anthony and I started our new life together. We were married October 20, 2001. Our wedding song—*Could not Ask For More* by Sara Evans—sums up our feelings now and forever.

This experience has taught me several things: love can come when you least expect it, love comes in unexpected ways, and if love between two people is meant to be, it will happen. They will find each other, even somewhere as vast as the Internet.

Paula and Anthony Birkholz
Austin, Texas

Love From AOL Tech Support

Laurie and Billy's Story

"The computer was new to me and I was becoming frustrated with it."

—Laurie

"Thank you for calling America Online; how can I help you?" Those are the words I heard right before my life changed for the better.

For the previous six months my life had been in turmoil. My dad had been diagnosed with pancreatic cancer and I had been taking care of him for months. I even quit my job to be with him. My marriage of 12 1/2 years was falling apart and I was afraid of what getting a divorce would do to my children. My life was filled with confusion, fear and grief.

On April 10, 1997 my dad passed away. My heart was torn to pieces but I noticed how the sun's rays were shooting through the clouds looking like a direct elevator to heaven. I knew my dad had taken that elevator. As I drove to the hospital where my father's lifeless body lay, I remembered him telling me, "Don't worry about putting flowers on my grave; put them in your house and whenever you look at them, think about me." He also always encouraged me to do the things that would make me happy.

A month later I filed for divorce and enrolled in college. I bought a computer to use for my homework but the computer was new to me and I was becoming frustrated with it. I called the AOL help number and that's when a masculine voice answered, thanking me for calling and asking how he

111

could help me. I explained my problem to him. The technical support man's name was Billy and we joked and chatted while he tried to figure out the problem. Eventually he asked me if I had any kids. "Why?" I asked suspiciously. He said that my problem was due to someone changing the parental controls without a password. I thanked him for his help and apologized for being short with him. He wished me well and hung up.

When I came home from school that night I found an e-mail from Billy. It contained a song and flowers. I was surprised but sent him a thank you note. We started talking on the computer every day after that and eventually I allowed him to call me.

Finally, one day Billy drove all the way from Jacksonville, Florida to Port St. Lucie to meet me. It was an emotional meeting. The moment we laid eyes on each other a flame ignited in both our hearts. His eyes flashed like blue-green jewels. I knew that my heart would pound right out of my chest. Then shyness dropped over us like a tent. When we recovered emotionally, we talked and talked and talked. We became best friends for a year and a half and were engaged for two years before we married.

When I look back I am amazed at how much my life has changed for the better. I look up at that same sunny sky and it smiles at me, blows a cool breeze across my face and says, "Life is good." Love is out there. It will find you if you have the courage to embrace life and do what will make you happy.

Laurie and Billy
Florida

Pattie and Michael
Miracle Marriage

Miracle Marriage

Pattie and Michael's Story

"I don't need a woman I can live with; I need a woman I can't live without."

—Michael

I'm not surprised that people find love on the Internet. There are lots of opportunities and possibilities for meeting that special someone. What's amazing to me, though, is the way my husband and I found each other on the Internet in May of 1999. It was nothing short of a miracle.

I was a 28-year-old divorcée with two kids, living with my parents after a painful divorce. To help occupy our time, I bought a computer and picked AOL for my Internet provider because I had used it on a friend's computer. I told my parents they could use my computer too. I gave them their own screen names and after showing them how to sign on I told them I'd demonstrate how to do a profile search so they could find people with similar interests for chatting.

"Maybe you can find a man," my dad joked.

I decided to go along with his joke and entered a search for a divorced male in Tennessee and picked 1966 for his year of birth because 33 is my favorite number. When the search was complete only one guy who came up was online. His name was Mike and I was glad he was the one who was online. His personal quote in his profile really intrigued me. He said, "I don't need a woman I can live with; I need a woman I can't live without."

I wanted to get to know him better and asked him to chat. He said, "Sure."

We started chatting and there was an immediate bond. We shared many of the same likes and dislikes, were in similar career fields (I am a nurse and he is a health and safety specialist), and could talk about anything. It was eerie. We agreed to be totally honest with one another and we were; we had nothing to lose.

It was May 18, 1999 when Michael and I first met online, and we met in person for the first time the Sunday of Memorial Day weekend. That's pretty quick, but we talked a lot online and on the phone before then. Still, I was wary. I had heard bad things about the Internet and people being stalked. I actually gave Michael my voicemail number in Kansas that I check remotely, just to be safe. He called me on that phone line for the first time and called nine times! When I called him back later at his home, I left my real work number. He called me back and we finally connected and talked for 20 minutes or so before I gave him my home number. That night we talked for hours and decided to meet.

I was excited and scared the day we met. I lessened my fears by telling myself that I knew more about him than any blind date I ever had and that we were meeting in a public place. In fact, Michael had insisted on meeting in a public place so I would be at ease. We met at Exit 23 off Interstate 81 at McDonalds—not a very romantic spot, but our time together was. We spent the day at a local park walking by the water and talking.

We met the next day too and this time Michael brought a picnic lunch and flowers for me. A few days later, on June 4, it was my 29th birthday and Michael sent a basket of flowers to my work.

I'm shy and will never forget our third date when Michael said, "If you don't kiss me I'm going to die!" I was terrified. I hadn't had a first kiss in 10 years, but I kissed him and it was great. By our fourth date I knew he was "the one." He later confessed to me that it was on the fourth date that he knew I was "the one." From our first date, we saw each other every weekend and talked on the phone or computer every day. We still haven't missed a day.

We dated for several months before I introduced Michael to my children as my boyfriend. Instead, I introduced him as a friend of my brother-in-law. One day my son said, "Mom, why don't you date that Mike guy; he's really cool." I was so happy because both of my kids loved Michael.

We got married in a simple ceremony April 29, 2000. My son walked me down the aisle and my daughter was my flower girl. Twenty months later we had a baby, Ethan, who looks just like his daddy. My mom later reminded me that I had gotten everything I prayed for: a good husband, a good home (Michael already owned one), to be able to stay home with my kids (I was the primary bread winner in my first marriage but now I was going to be a full-time housewife and mother), and a good father figure for my children. I got it all. All because I humored my father that day I was showing him how to use the Internet.

Pattie and Michael
Knoxville, Tennessee

Chapter Six

Additional Short Stories of Internet Love

Rockin' Into Love

My dream man answered my ad on Love@AOL. When I met this fella, it was at the local Cracker Barrel after talking for months and months online. We talked so long over dinner that we decided to leave and go outside so someone else could have our table. We sat on a couple of white rockers on the porch of the restaurant and talked for two solid hours. We are now hitched and a very loving couple. Guess what I got for our first anniversary? A rocker from Cracker Barrel. LOL.

Junior and Patricia Moore Jr.
Birmingham, Alabama

Instant Messages/Instant Love

In October 2000 I broke my leg and was home, alone and miserable. I went to a chat room for the first time and within minutes a guy typed, "Does anyone live in Glendale?" That was three miles from me so I said I did. We IM'd for about two minutes and he said he would bring me whatever I needed. I was so bored I said okay. About an hour later, a car pulled up in front of my house and the most handsome man got out. I was scared and excited all at once. What would he think? Was he a wacko or what, I wondered. He came in and was the kindest, warmest, most caring man I had ever met. It was instant love. We both knew we were the one for each other. We have spent every day together ever since and are now married. Dreams do come true and it only gets better.

Rachel Gorman

Pen pals to Partners

When I was a graduate student my brothers had AOL for easy Internet access for school projects. It was February of 1998 when Blueye466—or Michael—read my profile and sent me an e-mail asking if I wanted to be pen pals since we both lived in Tallahassee and newly divorced, he was looking for new friends. Although I was dating someone else at the time, I agreed to a platonic Internet relationship. Eventually I broke up with the guy I was dating. Michael asked me to call him and I did. Soon we were taking almost every night. A month later we met in person. We dated for two years and married in August 2000. We have joint custody of Michael's 7-year-old and had our first child in September of 2001. We are a happy family and I feel so blessed to have found my Mr. Right on AOL.

Lori and Michael
Tallahassee, Florida

Swimming with the Dolphins

I answered Mike's personal ad at our local Digital City in May of 1999 because he said he wanted to swim with the dolphins. We e-mailed for awhile, then IM'd, then talked on the phone. It turns out that he graduated a year behind me from a nearby school district and we had friends in common and never knew it. Our first five dates were ice cream trips to the local Whippi Dip, chaperoned by my boys, then two and four. We became best friends and Mike proposed in September 1999 and we were married a year later on the 24th. We are still best friends, a couple of love birds who love the family that we are. If I hadn't answered his ad, we might have walked right by each other and never known what we were missing.

Michael and Katie Wozny
Muskegon, Michigan

New Year's Miracle

New Year's Eve 2000, everyone was celebrating and welcoming in the new millennium but me. I was at home with a bottle of champagne to go along with my tears. I had just broken up with my fiance of a year and now I was all alone for the holidays. I was completely miserable and all I could think about was how and where I would finally find my true love, my soul mate, my partner. I felt as though I had searched everywhere and this latest relationship was my last hope.

A few nights later I was on the computer playing bingo and I got an IM from some guy. I decided to talk to him although that was unlike me. We instantly clicked. We chatted on the computer and the phone for a week and then he drove to meet me. Two months later we were married. The funny thing is that my husband told me right before we were married that the day we met on the computer he was playing around and his computer shut off for no reason, clicked back on again and my handle just popped up. Who says finding love on the Internet never works?

Dan and Shannon Orr

Windy City Connection

Michael and I met in a chat room November 2000. I asked everyone in the room where they were from and one of the responses was Chicago. I love Chicago. Being from a small town, I found it exciting.

From that moment on we chatted night after night for weeks, getting to know each other in the best way we could without meeting face to face.

When we were ready to meet in person we were both excited and scared. He came in on a train and told me to look for a guy with a red, white and blue leather coat, with USA printed on it.

The train arrived on schedule and I stood in the crowd searching for the owner of that jacket. He was one of the last people to get off the train and as he walked towards me with a huge smile on his face, I knew in an instant we would always be together. Now, we are engaged to get married. I have truly found the other part of me thanks to the Internet and the fact I love Chicago.

Michael Cosentino and Angela Padgett
Nappanee, Indiana

Bulletin Board Bride

I met my husband online almost seven years ago thanks to my 13-year-old son Neal's computer knowledge. My parents gave him a computer for Christmas 1991 and one day I checked on him and he was typing on a black screen with words scrolling on the bottom of the screen. I asked him what he was doing and he said he was talking to someone. I was shocked and worried and asked him to get off and explain the whole thing to me. He told me he was on a BBS, a bulletin board service in Sacramento. He told me that he dialed a number, then signed up to join a location on the computer where he could play games and talk to people. My concern turned to fascination and soon I had my own computer and was online every night. I met my husband about four months later.

We were both chatting in a common room and Phil asked if we could meet outside the computer world. We continued talking online for the next month and then met for lunch. We lingered for almost three hours, talking about our lives and dreams. We fell in love that day. Two years later we married in April of 1996. I believe that getting to know my best friend and husband online before meeting him in person was a benefit and I would not change a thing. He is the best thing that has ever happened to me.

Jessica Brown and Phil Mosca
Davis, California

Hearts Playing Heartthrob

When I bought my computer in May of 2000, I was fascinated with the idea of playing cards with people from all over the country. I played every night and had a great time talking with interesting, fun-loving people.

I was playing Hearts on Yahoo in June when I was invited to play cards with two guys from Louisiana (I lived in Connecticut). These Southern boys were funny—we had a blast and played until 4:00 a.m. "Milkman" was sweet and we seemed to have a lot in common. We exchanged e-mail addresses and said goodnight.

We continued to play cards as partners and e-mails turned into daily IMs on AOL. We chatted for hours and eventually called each other on the phone nightly. I went Yahoo for Milkman!

In mid August, I flew to Louisiana to meet him. My family and friends thought I was crazy but I just knew he was the man of my dreams. I stayed for five days and we cried when I left.

For the next two months, we talked nightly on the phone and decided we couldn't live without one another. In October, he came to Connecticut and we packed my belongings and drove to Louisiana. We have been blissfully happy ever since.

Carol Nechitilo and Brian
Alexandria, Louisiana

Instant Fit: Paradise

I met Ronda when we both placed an ad on Love@AOL. We had both been through rotten marriages and just wanted to make friends to do stuff with. We both enjoyed country music, going out to dinner and hiking. After several weeks of getting to know each other through IMs, we went on our first date. When I picked Ronda up that first night, I was nervous as a kid on his first date. I relaxed after we arrived at the Brazilian Grill where we were having dinner and we had a great time talking and getting to know each other. I loaned her my digital camera when she left a few days later for a six-day trip to San Francisco. When Ronda got back, we went hiking in the mountains and headed to my house where I cooked dinner for her and she met my three kids. They instantly hit it off and we started  calling this "our little family" right away. My daughter followed Ronda around like a little puppy and wanted to be with her 24/7. We got married May 5, 2001. Our wedding was a small family gathering in a log cabin at the Hill Air Force Base in Roy, Utah, not far from the Chemical Weapons Disposal Facility where I worked. On July 29, 2001 I was transferred to Maui, Hawaii where we will be for at least three and a half years. We were in Paradise before we even knew that I'd be stationed there.

Tim and Ronda Jones
Maui, Hawaii

0-595-24942-6